Praise for *Leadership*

"Bill has drawn on years of effe[...] book full of rich biblical insig[...] [...] suggestions so you can implement what you learn. Clearly written by someone who knows what he's talking about."

— Richard Blackaby, PhD, President of Blackaby Ministries International

"Bill is a very accomplished business leader who has studied these topics extensively. He does continual research and the presentation of his years of work and research are worth reading! The topics are as old as creation itself but his fresh approach is a treasure you will want to uncover."

— Dave Rae, Chief Operating Officer of Crown Financial Ministries

"The greatest lack among Christian leaders, including business leaders, is the lack of understanding of the scriptures and their application to everyday leadership issues. The Bible is the handbook that tells how the Kingdom of God works and leaders will lead inadequately if they are not leading through biblical principles. They must also have a strong prayer life to be strong leaders. Bill has addressed both these issues very well in this timely book. It is much needed if Christian leaders are to lead effectively for God's Kingdom, especially in the marketplace."

— William M. Moeny, President of Tetra Corporation

"Bill Bliss has put his finger on the very pulse of leadership. No matter how many books you have read on this subject, your learning will not be complete until you have read this book!"

— Joe Pellegrino, Publisher of Life & Leisure Newspapers

"Practical and biblical. *Leadership Lessons from THE BOOK* teaches the most crucial leadership lessons in one of the most thorough, simple, and functional forms I've ever read. If you are in a leadership position, *Leadership Lessons from THE BOOK* is sure to help you focus the way you lead, make decisions, and live your life."

— Jason Wilson, Executive Pastor of NewSpring Community Church

"Are you looking for practical biblical direction as you lead your organization? Bill Bliss has provided clear direction for hundreds of CEOs and helped them to communicate their vision. In this book, Bill uses the examples of Jesus, Nehemiah, Peter, and others to give us practical biblical counsel. Bill has been a tremendous help to our organization, our members, and hundreds of other business owners. His trusted experience and wisdom is now available for you in this book."

— Kent Humphreys, Ambassador of FCCI / Christ@Work, former CEO of Jack's, a leader in the distribution of consumer products

"In my years of ministry, I've never met a Christian in the marketplace who didn't want to understand better how God's Word related to their role at work. Yet I've seen few solid tools to help us – until now. In this book, Bill joins his deep experience in business consulting with a passion for pleasing Christ by following His Word. This book is practical, biblical, and real. If you want to walk with God at work, you should read and heed every chapter."

— Ken MacGillivray, Pastor of Hopevale Church

"Bill has succinctly captured the essence of what it takes to be a great leader. Not a great leader in the sense of the one with the most toys wins or the one with the biggest bank account and biggest everything else is the best. A great leader in the sense of one who lives their life knowing that when it's all over they have left far more on this earth than they took for the good of others and the glory of God. This book takes key biblical principles of leadership and puts them in one place. A great resource for anyone who wants to lead the right way. Bill hits the nail on the head with his chapter on Setting Expectations. He shows how clear God sets His expectations for us and then marries this concept to the world of today's leaders. I'm sold on his advice and will take immediate action by completing his suggested steps."

— Gary Williams, President of Coakley & Williams Hotel Management Company

"This is the most complete, inclusive and all encompassing roadmap of visioning that I have found. Not only is the vision-setting process made thoroughly clear, it explains the approach, guidelines and diplomacy necessary to position a vision for life-changing impact."

— Kip Miller, President and CEO of Eastern Industrial Supply

"Bill combines biblical wisdom, with his own practical experience to deliver useful, practical instruction. As I read the chapter on communication, I found myself saying, 'yes, that's right – I knew that' and at the same time realizing that I needed to use Bill's instruction as a road map to improve my own communication skills."

— **Charles Wall, Vice President and Regional Manager of Commercial Metals Company**

"In *Leadership Lessons From THE BOOK*, Bill gives dynamic leadership lessons rooted in God's word. He also provides the very practical and necessary steps for the application of these lessons for today's leader. This book is an important tool for us in our business, and I recommend it for any leader looking to grow personally and honor God in his or her organization. Thank you, Bill!"

— **Lee Mitchell, President of Applied Catalysts, Inc.**

"Offers profound and meaningful lessons into how biblical principles can transform leadership at every level. Bill has delivered a practical, genuinely useful book for leaders of all types of organizations."

— **Tony Morgan, Strategist, Coach, Writer, Speaker and Consultant who equips leaders and churches to impact their communities for Christ – www.TonyMorganLive.com**

"This book reflects Bill's passion for developing leaders to bring honor and glory to God. I love the connection he provides between biblical principles and their practical application to everyday leadership challenges. This book will help every single reader improve their level of leadership."

— **Joseph Sangl, Founder of I Was Broke. Now I'm Not.**

Leadership Lessons From
THE BOOK

Applying Biblical Lessons For Today's Leader

WILLIAM G BLISS

NIN Publishing
Anderson, South Carolina 29621 USA

Leadership Lessons From THE BOOK – Applying Biblical Lessons For Today's Leaders
Copyright © 2009 by William G Bliss

Published in Anderson, South Carolina, by NIN Publishing

Cover design by Chris Dunagan

Library of Congress Control Number: 2009934625

Bliss, William G.

ISBN 978-1-61623-028-9

First Edition

Printed in the United States by Morris Publishing
3212 East Highway 30
Kearney, NE 68847
1-800-650-7888

CONTENTS

In the beginning God created the heavens and the earth.
(Genesis 1:1)

Trust in the Lord with all your heart
and lean not on your own understanding;
in all your ways acknowledge him
and He will make your paths straight.
(Proverbs 3:5-6)

"All authority in heaven and on earth has been given to me.
Therefore go and make disciples of all the nations
baptizing them in the name of the Father, and of the Son
and of the Holy Spirit, and teaching them to obey
everything I have commanded you. And surely I am with
you always, to the very end of the age."
(Matthew 28:18-20)

PREFACE

We are in a time where the Christian leader is more out of touch with Scripture than at perhaps any other time in history. The secular world is placing a tremendous amount of pressure on organizational leaders of all types to follow their leadership methods and to turn their backs on God's methods. As Christian leaders, we are running the great risk of relying on the "wisdom" of the secular world instead of God's wisdom.

Proverbs 2 is clear about the requirement God places on us to consider carefully the sources from whom we obtain our wisdom; it spells out the consequences we will face if we fail to follow His wisdom. Consider verses 12-15 from this chapter: "Discretion will protect you and understanding will guard you. Wisdom will save you from the ways of wicked men, from men whose words are perverse, who leave the straight path to walk in dark ways, who delight in doing wrong and rejoice in the perverseness of evil, whose paths are crooked and who are devious in their ways." Does the description of wicked, evil, devious, perverse words remind you of the secular or worldly messages we are receiving today?

Jesus told us we cannot serve both God and mammon. In interpreting this guidance, mammon is not just a reference to money; it is a reference to operating in any way that is opposed to God's way. Jesus is simply saying we can not be focused on two directions at the same time.

Today, we are bombarded with messages attempting to take us away from living an integrated life as a Christian. The messages seem to say it might be acceptable to live as a Christian on Sunday, yet if you want to survive, thrive and otherwise prosper you had better get with the program (read – doing things the worldly way) or you will be a loser and a failure. The world wants us to focus on the short-term, temporal things that bring us (and those who sell things) pleasure. God clearly wants us to focus on long-term and Kingdom-building priorities that have an eternal impact. Jesus tells us not to store up treasures on earth. He commands us to store up treasures in heaven and to focus on these things, for the things we seek to store will drive our motives. Jesus clearly wants our motives to be focused on Him and not on what the world values. Jesus' rebuke of the Pharisees in Luke 16:15 is just as applicable to Christian leaders today – what the world honors is detestable to God.

A serious lack of Scriptural awareness is not new to God's people. His Word contains several examples of this happening during the period the Bible was written. Consider if the following verses could be applicable to us today:

- Isaiah 1:4 speaks of an "sinful nation" who have "forsaken the Lord" and who "have turned their backs on (the Lord)"
- In Nehemiah 8, after the wall has been completed the people gathered to hear a reading from the Book of the Law of God. Upon hearing the Law and considering their previous behavior of the past many years the people's reaction was to weep, in part because they now knew how sinful they were.
- Hosea 4:6 says, "…my people are destroyed from lack of knowledge".
- Proverbs 28:14 reads, "Blessed is the man who always fears the Lord, but he who hardens his heart falls into trouble."

Fearing the Lord is having deep awe, understanding and knowledge of who He is and what He requires of us. Jesus often called the Pharisees hypocrites; although they knew the "letter" of the Law, they put traditions and religious legalism ahead of following the Law. Outwardly, they might have given the impression that they 'feared' God, yet their motives and their heart were clearly aligned with those outward actions. This lack of Scriptural awareness earned them the sharpest rebuke given by Jesus.

In Henry and Richard Blackaby's devotional, *Discovering God's Daily Agenda*, they write, "The importance of God's Word cannot be overstated. If you are to serve the Lord in any capacity, you must know Scripture thoroughly. You must study it, meditate on it and obey it completely." This is not only great advice for today's Christian leader, it is imperative that we behave this way and commit to honor God by doing our best to understand His priorities for the leadership roles He has given us.

We must pray that God would permit us to see what He sees. As we actually become more familiar with the Scriptures, we will begin to see what is important to God. As this knowledge and insight take hold, we will begin to see how God desires for us to change our motives, beliefs, thoughts and actions to be more aligned with His purposes, especially in the organizations we lead.

God has not called us into leadership positions to be part time Christians and part time leaders. He has called us because He desires to accomplish an important work through us as fully committed and empowered Christian leaders. In Romans 1:16 Paul says he is not ashamed of talking about Jesus. If we are part time Christians and full time leaders, we might tend to hold back in speaking about Him.

God has gifted us to do this combined work as Christians AND leaders and provided all we need to carry it out (see Ephesians 2:10). To enhance our Scriptural awareness, we must commit to understand His desires and His purposes and resolve to obey them. James 1:22 tells us to not just listen or read the Word, but to obey what it says. If we just listen without doing, we are just fooling ourselves.

Allow me to paraphrase Esther 4:14-15. For if you, the Christian leader, remain silent at this time, relief and deliverance for God's people will arise from another place, (for His purposes will prevail) but you and your family (and your organization) will perish. Have you been appointed to this leadership position for a time such as this?

Leadership Lessons From THE BOOK

In Fall 2008, a survey of leadership development practices was conducted by our company (Bliss & Associates Inc) and approximately 600 Christian leaders and CEOs responded. Some of the key findings include:

1. While acknowledging the importance of leadership development to their organization's success, many respondents seem to struggle with the attention they provide to leadership development efforts. Without planned leadership development, organizations might not be adequately prepared for the leadership challenges (vision setting, directional unity, motivation, focus, employee engagement, etc.) they will likely face in the months and years to come.

2. Succession planning – usually viewed as an absolute necessity at secular companies – seems to be something that many respondents in this survey do not adequately address. It appears that these business leaders have not adequately thought through the potential problems someone would face if they were somehow incapacitated, not to mention the significant impact their incapacitation would have on many other lives.

3. There seems to be an expressed desire to learn how to create a succession plan. An effective succession plan is really not that difficult or time consuming to create. What can be difficult is having an objective and quantifiable method to assess potential replacement candidates.

4. Many of the companies would be interested in learning more about how to develop leadership competencies as well as having an objective assessment of its leaders against those competencies.

5. Although a vast majority of leaders use the "informal feedback" approach to provide feedback to their executive team, they might benefit from taking more active and planned approaches to providing feedback that would help drive desired results. This has been validated by the respondents in their strong expression of desired training in providing performance feedback.

6. As indicated in the comments that respondents have provided, many are crying out for distinctively Christian tools, approaches and methods to help them run their organizations that go beyond the current offerings that seem to be available.

Throughout this book, I will reference some specific results from this survey. Although the results or implications were not necessarily the primary motivation for writing this book, they did call out the need for practical leadership development tools, methods and techniques that are aligned with God's Word and can be utilized by today's leaders.

This is not just another book on leadership; it is a book focused on key leadership lessons found in God's Word along with how today's leader can immediately apply some of those lessons in their organization. The Bible is loaded with verses that are applicable to leadership.

Leadership Lessons from THE BOOK provides an in-depth discussion of seven leadership lessons found in God's Word. It is not meant to be an exhaustive all-inclusive list of leadership lessons or principles, merely those that are among the most important. Each chapter addresses a lesson, and the chapters are formatted as follows:

- *Scripture Passages* Three or four verses highlighting the lesson
- *Biblical Foundation* An in-depth discussion of what the Bible says about that lesson
- *Lessons Learned* A summary of what the Bible says about that lesson

- *Practical Application* A discussion of that lesson relevant for today's leader
- *Self Assessment* In some chapters, a brief self assessment is provided to help the reader gauge his/her proficiency of that lesson
- *Practical Steps to Exhibit* Provides a dozen or more steps that can be put into action by today's leader.

We will explore some key leadership verses including:
- One day soon afterward Jesus went up on a mountain to pray, and he prayed to God all night. At daybreak, he called together all of his disciples and chose twelve of them to be apostles. (Luke 6:12-13, NLT)
- Where there is no vision, the people are unrestrained. (Proverbs 29:18, NASB)
- You have heard me teach things that have been confirmed by many reliable witnesses. Now teach these truths to other trustworthy people who will be able to pass them on to others. (II Timothy 2:2, NLT)
- Simply let your yes be yes and your no be no; anything beyond this comes from the evil one. (Matthew 5:37)
- You know that the rulers in this world lord it over their people, and officials flaunt their authority over those under them. But among you it will be different. (Matthew 20:25-26, NLT)

Before beginning each chapter, I suggest that you pray and ask the Holy Spirit to open the eyes of your heart and mind so He can direct you to what He wants you to understand. This is a crucial step in ensuring that your mind and heart are ready to receive what the Holy Spirit wants you to learn. He is able to tell you things that are very specific to you and remind you of things that are beneficial for you.

Additionally, I suggest that as you read each chapter underline or highlight key points made in each of the sections. Alternatively you might want to have a pen and notebook or journal handy to record any insights you may discover. In the chapters that contain a *Self Assessment* section, take the time to complete the assessment. It will guide you in identifying some of the *Practical Steps* you might want to consider taking to enhance your skills and behaviors in that particular leadership lesson. When you arrive at the *Practical Steps* section at the end of each chapter, identify two or three steps that seem to be best for you or your organization during this season. With more than one hundred twenty practical steps listed in this book, wait until you complete the book to decide which steps you will implement; then review the list of items you have selected throughout each chapter. Select the two or three most impactful steps and develop a plan to accomplish those first. Then move on to others as time permits and as you see the fruit from the initial steps.

As you finish the book and reflect on the topics discussed, you might want to share this with your leadership team. I invite you to review the material included in the back of the book for information about workshops and study guides available for that very purpose.

My prayer for each reader of this book is two fold. For those who are currently a serious student of Scripture, I pray this book will provide encouragement to you to continue in your daily habits to immerse yourself in reading, absorbing, meditating and practicing the wisdom that God's Word so richly provides on the topic of leadership. For those who discover they need a deeper awareness and knowledge of what God has said about His leadership model and expectations of a Christian leader, my prayer is that you would commit yourself to begin this serious, life-changing journey without delay or interruption. Additionally, my prayer for each reader is that they hear the words, "Well done, good and faithful servant" when each of you finally go home to be with the Lord.

===

CHAPTER ONE

===

SETTING A VISION

Without vision, the people perish

Scripture Passages

- "For the Son of Man came to seek and save those who are lost." (Luke 19:10 NLT)
- "Then I said to them, 'You see the trouble we are in: Jerusalem lies in ruins, and its gates have been burned with fire. Come let us rebuild the wall of Jerusalem, and we will no longer be in disgrace.' " (Nehemiah 2:17)
- Where there is no vision, the people are unrestrained. (Proverbs 29:18 NASB)

Leadership Lessons From THE BOOK

Introduction

Why do some organizations seem to continually grow, prosper and have a positive impact on their community while others flounder, lose money and employees, lose respect and eventually close their doors? Obviously, there can be many explanations. One of the surest explanations has to do with vision; either a lack of a vision, lack of commitment to that vision or lack of clarity of the vision.

Setting a vision provides the foundation and core values for everything you do personally and professionally. Companies or organizations without vision are like sailboats without rudders; they blow wherever the wind takes them. Without a vision, they can be heavily influenced and directed by the marketplace's changing patterns. They tend to be reactive and not proactive.

Leaders at organizations without a strong vision do their own thing with little connection to the company's main purpose. These leaders, not to mention employees, often feel frustrated, disconnected, and unappreciated. Setting a vision and regularly reminding employees of that vision allows them to stay engaged, connected and contributes to their motivation to perform. It enables them to see and have a purpose in their work.

Establishing and communicating a vision provides the building blocks of leadership. It enables leaders to speak to, guide and direct their staff with purpose and resolve. It allows leaders to establish measurements of progress. It enables leaders to set clear goals that drive people and the organization in a specific direction to accomplish a desired result or outcome. Vision provides an essential ingredient to employee motivation.

Effective leaders spend a great deal of time thinking through what the vision ought to be, how to make it compelling so others will be energized by it, and how to reinforce it and keep it top of mind among staff. They do not rush into it nor do they take on this critical assignment on their own. They engage with others to provide input, dissect, tear apart and otherwise reconstruct the vision to ensure the outcome is clear, concise and passionate. Most importantly, effective leaders strive to have a vision that is larger than they are as individuals. As Christian leaders, they strive to have a vision that has an Eternal and Kingdom-focused impact.

What does Scripture tell us about setting a vision? It turns out, Scripture says a lot. Let us learn from Jesus and Nehemiah, both visionary leaders in tough times.

Biblical Foundation

Jesus received what we might call the Ultimate Vision in heaven, communicated it on earth for the three years of His public ministry and changed the world forever. He is our best model for establishing and communicating a vision.

Sometime before creation, the Father, Son and Spirit consulted regarding their highest creation – us. Knowing we would rebel against Him, God decided how He would make it possible to reconcile us and also satisfy His justice. God would prepare the way for the coming of the Son through illustrations, prophecies and a close relationship with one nation of people. At just the right time, the Father would send the Son to be the Savior of the world. The Son would become human through a poor Jewish virgin, live a sinless life and die as the complete payment for all the offenses of mankind.

The Father would bring His Son back to life to demonstrate His approval of the Son's payment and exalt Him to heaven's highest place. The Father and Son would send the Spirit to convict people of their rebellion against God, convince them of their hopelessness without Christ, and invite them to receive Him as Savior and Lord.

When Jesus came to earth, He knew why He was here and what He needed to do to accomplish the vision. Every decision and every action had purpose and helped fulfill the vision. His Father twice expressed His pleasure with the progress Jesus was making toward fulfilling the mission. Just before Jesus succumbed to the crucifixion, He could say with integrity, *Tetelestai!* (It [Jesus' saving mission] has been accomplished!).

3

Wouldn't it be great for God to give you that kind of vision for your organization or career? He actually has given the Christian leader the vision He desires for us to accomplish. He has given us His complete revelation, the Bible. Instead of giving His advice on one or two life decisions, God provided the whole manual for living. He instilled His certified teacher in our hearts, the Holy Spirit, and connected us with His body, the church. We have so much going for us in establishing our vision.

How did Jesus communicate His vision so men and women felt compelled to give their lives (sometimes literally) to it? He stated it concisely, creatively and compellingly. Jesus concisely stated His vision several times. People took notice. "I have come that they might have life." (John 10:10) "I have come to seek and save the lost." (Luke 19:10) "The Son of Man did not come to be served but to serve and to give His life." (Mark 10:44) "I came to do the will of Him who sent me." (John 4:34)

Jesus' creativity knew no bounds. He knew how to speak to His audience on their own terms. To fishermen, He talked about fishing. To a woman beside a well, He talked about living water. To a biblical scholar, He talked about the mysterious work of the Spirit. Jesus used common, contextual topics to challenge people to an uncommon understanding. That understanding was necessary for Jesus to engage others to accomplish His vision.

Jesus' concise, creative statements of His vision compelled many to follow Him – and some to walk away. He invited Peter and Andrew to "Come, follow me and I will make you fishers of men." Shortly after, He called James and John. Scripture shows how compelling His statement was: "At once, they left their nets and followed him … Immediately they left the boat and their father and followed Him." (Matthew 4:18-22) When public opinion turned sour, Jesus asked His followers if they also would leave Him. Their answer? "To whom will we go, you have the words of eternal life" (John 6:68).

Peter's response to Jesus after His resurrection is perhaps the greatest indication of how compelling Jesus' vision was to him and the other disciples. Peter had seen the Lord arrested, beaten and crucified. Peter saw it firsthand and he was not known for his attraction to pain. The risen Lord predicted that

Peter would be killed for following the Savior and then said simply, "Follow me." Jesus and His vision were so compelling, Peter had only one logical choice – to risk life and limb and follow Jesus (See John 21:15-23).

People certainly opposed Jesus' vision. He faced opposition nearly every day of His public ministry. Many people *did* believe in Him and His vision (as much as they understood it at the time), yet many felt threatened. After all, if all the people became followers of Christ, what would the religious leaders do? People would not seek (or pay for) *their* instruction. Most significant, their authority would be questioned and their pursuit of status and position stymied.

Occasionally, Jesus' immediate staff, His chosen twelve, opposed His vision and plans. At other times, they tried to suggest revisions. When Jesus began to predict His coming death, Peter rebuked Him in front of the other apostles: "Never Lord! This shall never happen to you." (Matthew 16:22). Jesus' closest friends sometimes misunderstood and opposed His vision. Despite all this opposition, Jesus never strayed from it. He never compromised or altered it to appease the opposition, His staff or His followers.

Jesus regularly reminded people of His vision. He took the opportunity to recast the same vision over and over again so His followers would be able to really capture its meaning, purpose and passion. This was necessary because as a leader, Jesus knew the vision would be carried out long after He was gone. His key followers had to have complete clarity of that vision if they were to carry it out as Jesus intended. Notice that through the years, people have added their own spin to His vision which has resulted in an argument about whose version is right as opposed to doing the work to accomplish the vision.

Nehemiah exemplifies a model visionary. This Jewish POW served as cupbearer to Artaxerxes, King of Persia, about 450 B.C. His nation (Judah) and beloved capital (Jerusalem) lay in ruins, inhabited by the poor remnants of devastating wars. Nehemiah now lived far from the devastation and held an enviable position in King Artaxerxes' court. As cupbearer, kings chose their most trusted servants to taste all their food and drink to avoid assassination by poisoning. King Artaxerxes trusted Nehemiah with his life.

Nehemiah's relative and others updated him on the status of his fellow Jews and the city of Jerusalem: "They said to me, 'Those who survived the exile and are back in the province are in great trouble and disgrace. The wall of Jerusalem is broken down, and its gates have been burned with fire.' When I heard these things, I sat down and wept. For some days I mourned and fasted and prayed before the God of heaven." (Nehemiah 1:3-4)

Bruce Wilkinson and Chip Ingram (Bible teachers) observe that leaders who set a vision have a passion, commitment and ownership of their vision before they make it public. Nehemiah worked out his vision to rebuild the wall with God before approaching King Artaxerxes. When he spoke to the king, he had specific plans that would fulfill his vision. He knew that the king could provide the financial support for the materials needed. This might have been the first recorded business plan presented to a major funding source!

Although the Bible does not specifically state it, Nehemiah must have developed quite a strong relationship with the king. Think about it. The king was not a Jew and probably cared little about the Jews beyond political expedience, but He did have some level of compassion for Nehemiah and what his fellow Jews were experiencing. Why else would he grant Nehemiah a paid leave of absence to address a problem located geographically outside the king's realm? Developing trust with the people you need to help you is an important lesson in leadership. Waiting until you need their help is not the time to begin building that trust.

Nehemiah sharpened his vision when he arrived in Jerusalem. First, he assessed the situation alone, at night, gathering firsthand information about the task ahead. He took a full tour of the wall and various gates to assess their exact condition. After making his own assessment, he assembled the workers, the priests and others who needed to know about his plan.

" 'You see the trouble we are in: Jerusalem lies in ruins, and its gates have been burned with fire. Come, let us rebuild the wall of Jerusalem, and we will no longer be in disgrace.' I also told them about the gracious hand of my God upon me and what the king had said to me." (Nehemiah 2:17-18a)

He stated his vision concisely, creatively and compellingly – "Come, let us rebuild the wall of Jerusalem, and we will no longer be in disgrace." Their response? "Let's start rebuilding" (2:18b). This began the transition of a vision to a mission – a clear outline of what must be done to realize or accomplish the vision.

As all visions do, Nehemiah's encountered opposition. Powerful local leaders named Sanballat, Tobiah and Geshem teamed up to mock and ridicule Nehemiah. They plotted together to fight against Jerusalem, which prompted Nehemiah to prepare his men to fight while continuing to rebuild the wall. Nehemiah not only had opposition to his vision, he had to alter his strategies so the vision would be protected. The alteration came in the form of preparing his men to fight while continuing their primary purpose of rebuilding.

When the oppositional leaders' plot failed with the completion of the wall, the three enemies tried to lure Nehemiah out of the city. He saw through their plot and refused. Opposition to Nehemiah's vision was fierce, but he focused on it, thwarted the opposition and succeeded.

Lessons Learned about Setting a Vision

1. A vision needs a visionary – one who models, articulates and protects the vision.
2. A vision often seems impossible to achieve.
3. A vision must be communicated concisely, creatively and compellingly to stir others' commitment to it.
4. A vision primarily serves the needs of others, not the needs of the leader.
5. A worthwhile vision must have an eternal – not just temporal – impact.
6. A vision will be opposed.

A vision needs a visionary – one who models, articulates and protects the vision.

No vision survives without a visionary – someone who just will not let it go. A leader must be the person others look to for the clearest explanation and embodiment of the vision. Jesus not only talked about serving others, but He also served others. He not only preached humility before God, but He also prayed, "Not my will, but your will be done." Nehemiah not only recognized that somebody needed to organize resources and obtain permission to rebuild the walls of Jerusalem, but he also risked life and limb to lead the effort. Do not settle for "we should" meetings. Effective leaders are the champion of their vision and when this happens others will catch it.

A vision often seems impossible to achieve.

Both Jesus' and Nehemiah's visions fall into the audacious category. God's vision for His Son was to save the world, not just some of it. Not just a few people, but the entire world. No one else could or would have made the claim that they had come to save the world. Yet, one must have confidence that they can achieve the vision. In this case, Jesus was the only one who could possibly achieve this vision, and He accomplished the exclusive provision for it.

Nehemiah envisioned rebuilding Jerusalem's ruined walls and gates to remove the disgrace of the Jewish nation.

Other people knew the walls and gates needed to be rebuilt. Some might have calculated the material and manpower needed to accomplish the task. No one until Nehemiah, however, rallied others to that vision because it seemed impossible.

A vision must be communicated concisely, creatively and compellingly to stir others' commitment to it.

The chapter on *Communication* explores the necessity of a sender being clear and concise. This applies especially in communicating a vision. A leader's vision must be communicated in ways that followers can understand, and easily remember and repeat to others. Jesus said it clearly and concisely: To save the world. Nehemiah said it clearly and concisely: To rebuild the wall. These simple vision statements leave little room for misunderstanding. These statements do not need to include how to accomplish it – just what the final outcome will be.

Jesus and Nehemiah also communicated their visions compellingly. They knew their audiences. They knew how to gain their attention and the words to use to ensure people knew they were serious about the end result. Jesus' immediate audience was the people of Israel. They were waiting for the Messiah to come and save them. The Scriptures had said, prefigured, and symbolized that fact for nearly 1500 years. Think about it: Jesus knew each of the apostles He called and communicated His vision to each one of them in a manner that spoke to them. Only to the fisherman did Jesus say, "I will make you fishers of men."

Nehemiah also knew his audience, be it the king who he had to convince to let him take a leave of absence and supply all the resources needed or the people who would actually rebuild the wall. He knew what it was going to take to gain their commitment. Nehemiah gained people's attention by telling them something they already knew: that they were in trouble and the wall was a disgrace. The residents knew they were vulnerable to attack because the wall did not offer them the physical protection it once had.

9

In the same way, a leader's vision must gain the commitment of their audience. Without commitment, the followers can easily become distracted, disinterested or unmotivated to complete their portion of the assignment. Jesus said it well: " 'Whoever does not believe stands condemned already because he has not believed in the name of God's one and only Son.' " (John 3:18b) Now that will capture anybody's attention.

A vision primarily serves the needs of others, not the needs of the leader.

This point is obvious when we think of Jesus and Nehemiah. Not so obvious when we look at organizations today. Both Jesus and Nehemiah stated their vision in terms that helped others, not themselves. Jesus came from eternity to earth not for His own benefit. As we will explore in the chapter on *Servant Leadership*, He came as a servant to the Father and as a servant to us. All that He did benefited others, not Him. Think about it, God the Father willed that His one and only Son save the world. Jesus served His Father. He also served people because there was no other way that we could receive forgiveness of sins, salvation and eternal life unless a perfect sacrifice was offered.

Nehemiah had a great job as cupbearer. The king protected him. His job was pretty well defined, had some risk, but had a lot of benefits. It was probably a pretty comfortable job with a lot of job security, as long as the king remained alive! The role of rebuilding the wall, where there was considerable danger and outside opposition, involved serving others and not Nehemiah's own needs.

A worthwhile vision must have an eternal, not just temporal, impact.

The end result of Jesus' and Nehemiah's visions would have a lasting impact on many people. Here is a good litmus test for a vision: Ask whether the vision will survive after the leader is gone. If the answer is, "No," rethink the vision. Even though your vision might not last for an eternity, it will probably not honor God if it only lasts for your lifetime, even if you are a small entrepreneur. Jesus' vision was an eternal vision. This is our model. If the vision is all about what you alone can accomplish, God does not receive the glory when it is accomplished. If it is a vision that can be accomplished by you, it is definitely not a God-sized vision.

Our vision should align with our values as a Christian. Many times, we are asked to participate in business or organizational goals that might conflict with our Christian values. Jesus and Nehemiah are wonderful role models of living consistent with their values as servants of Almighty God.

A vision will be opposed.

Both Jesus and Nehemiah encountered significant opposition from the people they were trying to influence in sharing their vision. The various opposition points and how both dealt with it have been discussed. First, they expected it to happen. Next, they did not ignore it when faced with it. They took it head on and dealt with the opposition immediately. Jesus had opposition every single day of His three year public ministry. He had opposition from His enemies, countrymen and even, on occasion, from His disciples.

Nehemiah had opposition from the ones who did not want the wall to be rebuilt. They wanted to have their own needs met by being able to defeat and control those people who lived within the broken down walls of Jerusalem. He also faced opposition from his workers when the work became overwhelming. He recognized this and overcame it.

Practical Application

Setting a vision is critical to our success in any aspect of life, yet few of us make the effort. As Christians, we know that we should live within the will of God. He tells us several times, "Be holy because I am holy." He has more in mind than attending church on Sundays. We also realize God has a unique and specific plan for our lives (see Jeremiah 29:11). Having a plan is a concept that comes from God. It is not a 'tool' created by a business school. God has filled the Bible with accounts of His plans for specific people. People succeeded or failed based upon their alignment with God's plans and the way they carried out His plans. Do you want to carry out God's plan for you as a leader who He has appointed for a time such as this?

Having the desire to establish a new vision for yourself or your organization assumes that you are dissatisfied with the status quo, that you believe that you, your team, your department or organization can achieve goals greater and more important than those presently planned or sought in the past. We have to be careful at this stage to ensure we know for certain that God is the one who is leading us to have this new vision and it is not of our own creation. Anything else and we run the risk of the vision being born from our own self-centeredness, pride or arrogance.

Dissatisfaction with the status quo can be healthy or unhealthy, stimulating growth or stifling it. If you are always dissatisfied, rarely celebrate or recognize achievements, or are overly focused on the next mile marker, your followers will lose heart and you will probably lose them. Casting vision means you understand the status quo, appreciate present strengths and successes and help people see the future potential. Naturally, as Christians, we want to focus on things that have an eternal impact or perspective, not limiting ourselves to only earthly, temporal goals.

Our vision for the organization might not have obvious eternal value. It should, however, be able to stand the test of some time and be of value to many (shareholders, customers, employees, vendors, etc.), not just a few individuals. As

Christian leaders, we are called to have the act of sharing the gospel with others as part of our vision.

What is God's vision for your department or organization? Have you ever thought about that? It matters for this reason – the earth is the Lord's and everything in it. (Psalm 24:1) God is as much involved with what happens on Monday through Friday in Fortune 500 companies, entrepreneurial start-ups and faith-based organizations as He is with your church on Sunday morning. Both include His highest creation – people.

The verse from Proverbs has a wealth of value as well. Although it is not referencing a particular event, the counsel is wise, useful and very relevant. Leaders, as well as the people they lead, need a vision. They need something that can motivate them to work long hours, go the extra mile, put in extra effort and take appropriate risks. If there is no vision, people are left to their own devices. In today's corporate parlance, this is called having personal agendas and silo thinking which leads to significant organizational dysfunction.

Even if you lead or manage an organization with five employees, God has a plan for that organization, and you are part of it. If you as a Christian leader are committed to having a Kingdom impact on the organization and the community, then your vision must extend beyond your position and the time you have in your position. Your vision must include having an impact that goes beyond you. You must be a Christian leader to your employees and by extension, their families. You must be a leader to your vendors and your customers.

"Plans go wrong for lack of advice; many advisors bring success." (Proverbs 15:22 NLT) This verse explains that the best vision develops among leaders, not within one leader. Sure, one of you may initiate, but others refine, define, supplement, and the resulting vision can be better than what you started with. The key lesson here is to develop vision in community with others who can provide perspective, assistance, and objective advice.

What then does a successful vision comprise? A successful vision comprises a clear vision statement, a mission, a set of core values, objectives and goals that clearly articulate what you are trying to accomplish. Let us define these terms.

Mission   This is a statement that defines where the organization, department or individual is supposed to place their focus. This is not a specific list of tasks or responsibilities, rather a broad statement of purpose. See if you remember this mission statement:

To explore strange new worlds; to seek out new life and new civilizations; to boldly go where no man has gone before.

Granted, this might be a silly example, yet it proves the point of clarity. Captain James T. Kirk of the Starship Enterprise proclaimed this mission statement each week as a new episode of Star Trek appeared on our television screens. Everyone who watched this show knew the spaceship's mission. The viewers (as well as the crew of the Enterprise) did not know what specific event was going to unfold for them, but they knew the overall mission, or purpose, of their journey. By beginning each episode with a reciting of the mission statement, we were all reminded of the main purpose. If we did not want to partake in this particular mission, we could switch channels.

Fellowship of Companies for Christ International is an organization that ministers to Christian Business leaders. Their mission statement says, "In pursuit of Christ's eternal objectives, we equip and encourage company leaders to operate their businesses and conduct their personal lives according to biblical principles." Read that again. Their purpose is so clear; the reader knows where they are putting the focus. It is not saying how they are going to equip and encourage, just that they will.

In John 1, we read the account of John the Baptist. The Jewish leaders were asking him to identify his purpose or mission. Since he was baptizing people, the leaders wanted to know who he was and why he was baptizing. John immediately said he was not the Messiah (v 20). They asked if he was Elijah or the prophet they were expecting. He replied, "No", to each question. Instead of saying who he was or giving a position title, he responded with his purpose. He quoted Isaiah: "I am a voice shouting in the wilderness, 'Clear a way for the Lord's coming!' " John the Baptist's purpose was not about who he was, but what he was called to do. Mission or purpose statements must be about what we are, not about who we are.

God explained the mission of Jesus for us and it is recorded in John 3:17, "For God did not send His Son in to the world to condemn the world, but to save the world through him." Simple and focused.

Mission statements should provide the answer to such questions as:

- *What is the reason this organization or department exists?* The Ritz Carlton hotel organization has a simple mission statement, "We are ladies and gentlemen serving ladies and gentlemen." The church where my wife and I are members states their reason for existence as, "To make the name of Jesus Christ famous, one life at a time."
- *For individuals the question is, "How do I fulfill my purpose"?* Do you have a personal mission statement? You might want to consider having one that will help guide you as to how you spend your time.
- *Who is my customer?* The answer helps focus marketing, sales, research, product development and other efforts to a specific customer cluster. Are your customers consumers or other businesses? If you run a restaurant, is your customer a fine diner who will spend money to be served expertly prepared meals or are they more interested in quick service for a reasonable price? The answer makes quite a difference in how the company is operated.
- *What makes my product or service different from others?* Without some sort of differentiation, your product or service becomes a commodity. With differentiation, your product or service has unique features only you can offer your targeted customers. Are your products focused on price, quality, value, selection, availability, variety or some combination of these?

- *What need am I serving by fulfilling this mission?* This helps employees become connected and engaged with the organization's purpose and also helps prioritize new initiatives. This question also helps to ensure the vision serves others and not the leader.

Christians can expand the mission statement by answering the question of how this organization or department fulfills the plan God has for their life and how living out this plan will have an eternal impact. "For we are God's workmanship, created in Christ Jesus to do good works, which God prepared in advance for us to do." (Ephesians 2:10) God has specific work that He planned for each of us long ago. It is safe to assume that God had an eternal purpose in mind, especially if He planned this work such a long time ago.

Additionally, as John 15 tells us, our task is to produce lasting fruit. One of the ways of determining if our fruit is lasting is to see if it has caused lives to be transformed. Recall in I Kings 19 when God asked Elijah, "What are you doing here?" The answer to this, based on quiet time and prayer with God, will help define our purpose for both our lives as individuals and for the organization we lead.

Core Values This is simply a statement of the operating philosophy of the organization. Also called "Words We Live By", "Guiding Principles", "Culture", or "Standards of Conduct", these core values do exactly what they say. They guide us with solid principles of behavior and provide a roadmap to follow in accomplishing the mission. Effective leaders emphasize the importance of their core values in carrying out the mission. Many describe them as an "accountability factor." Employees are encouraged to keep management accountable if they see management acting against one of the core values. A more complete exploration of core values is presented in the *Setting Expectations* chapter.

Objectives   These are statements of longer-term actions that support the vision and mission statements. They give clarity of action; they set priorities and define desired outcomes. Without priorities, employees would be left on their own to do what they thought was right or important. Many people use the terms 'goals' and 'objectives' interchangeably. They really have separate and distinct meanings. Objectives are directional in their reach, whereas goals are specific to the accomplishment of the objective.

Goals   These are statements of actions or tasks that must be carried out to accomplish the objectives. You might wish to utilize the acronym SMART in defining your goals. This acronym stands for:

- **S**pecific – Goals are precise, detailed and explicit.
- **M**easurable – A goal has quantifiable measures of performance so you know when it has been accomplished.
- **A**chievable – Goals are practical given the environment of the current situation; they are achievable within a reasonable period of time.
- **R**elevant – Goals must be relevant to the mission of the organization. If not, resources are being utilized that are not going to accomplish the mission.
- **T**ime-bound – Goals have a targeted completion date.

Goals must also be written, or they are just ideas without actionable plans.

Establishing a vision for a department or organization is one of the most important challenges and opportunities for a leader. Setting a worthwhile vision requires time to effectively craft and articulate, obtain input from others, gain commitment from all and achieve clarity in explanation and execution. If you are ready to tackle it, here is a suggested approach:

1. **Pray first**

    As we will learn in the next chapter, *Quiet Time and Prayer,* and as Jesus and Nehemiah have demonstrated to us, we should pray before beginning any significant endeavor. Unfortunately, most of the time we plan and then maybe we try to commit those plans to God by praying about them. Scripture is clear in that God is telling us to pray first and then plan with the insight He provides. You have probably heard the quip, "If you want to make God laugh tell Him your plans". Proverbs 16:3 tells us to "Commit your actions to the Lord and your plans will succeed."

2. **Set aside the right amount of time**
   How much time? It depends on the size of the organization and whether you are creating it from scratch or reviewing an existing one for continued relevancy. If the vision will guide a multilevel organization, such as a Fortune 500 organization, you might need up to six months. If you are establishing a new vision for a smaller organization of 100 employees, you still might take several months. If you are aligning a department or divisional vision with an existing corporate vision, it might take a month or two. Whatever time is required, understand that a worthwhile vision is not established at a typical one- or two-hour staff meeting.

3. **Assemble a team of advisors**
   The challenge of developing a vision for your organization, no matter how small or large, should not be one you take on alone. As Proverbs 15:22 teaches, it is wise to develop the vision among leaders and not with one leader. Ideally, your team of advisors will be a group of people who can champion the vision's components, namely its mission, core values, objectives and goals. Your direct staff of people who will implement the vision might be part of this team or you might choose to have an external team of people who know the broad environment and marketplace. It is helpful to arrange for the meeting to happen at an offsite location. This allows the people attending to focus on this critical task and not be interrupted by their normal work activities.

4. **Engage some outside help**

Even the most skilled leaders find it difficult, if not impossible, to facilitate a visioning session and be a participant at the same time. If your organization has a strong training or executive development function, perhaps someone on that staff can facilitate. If not, hire someone who has the expertise to help. It will be one of the wisest investments you will make.

5. **Take time to consider your ideas**

As you work to put the meat around the bones of mission, core values, objectives and goals, take time to reflect and meditate on what you are developing. This is the time to ask the Lord for His blessing on your work, to let these proposed plans take time to germinate and to see if this really is where the Lord is leading you and the organization.

6. **Communicate your vision to all concerned**

What good is your vision if your people do not know their roles in fulfilling it? This means that you must develop plans to communicate this vision to employees, customers, vendors and others who will have an impact on its accomplishment. Holding one big roll-out meeting to communicate it is not nearly enough. Actually, if you communicate this only once, it probably will not succeed. Your plan must include regular (usually monthly or quarterly at a minimum) updates to everyone so progress can be tracked and rewarded. Recall that Jesus took many opportunities to communicate His vision to people who had heard it before. This was to remind and encourage them to continue on, especially when faced with obstacles or setbacks.

7. **Establish accountability and measurements**

Plans devoid of responsibility or accountability will not be accomplished. This seems like such an obvious statement, yet many organizations fail to take this step. Their worthwhile vision withers from neglect, and "the way we have always done it" continues unchecked. Similarly, if you do not look at checkpoints along the way, how will you know if you are on the right path to reach your vision? Measurements help people deliver what is expected of them when such measurements are clear and objective. Remember, you can not expect what you do not inspect; if you do not measure it, you can not manage it.

Setting a vision is one of the foundational elements of ensuring a successful organization. For the Christian leader, this means following principles that God has established as essential. His process has proven again and again that it is successful. The roadmap is there; we merely need to follow it.

Setting A Vision

Self Assessment

Below are twenty statements that are indicative of an organization, department or leader who has a clear vision for their organization or role within the organization. As you read the statements, be aware of the first response that comes to mind as it applies to you or the organization and circle the number in the appropriate column.

Never – 1	Seldom – 2	Sometimes – 3	Usually – 4	Always – 5

1. Our vision, mission and core values are known by all employees.

    1   2   3   4   5

2. We have regular town hall or similar meetings where the vision and mission are openly discussed.

    1   2   3   4   5

3. I am aware of the specific points or people who oppose or are likely to oppose my vision.

    1   2   3   4   5

4. We have a process whereby employees can hold leaders accountable for their behavior, especially when that behavior might seem to go against our core values.

    1   2   3   4   5

5. Our objectives and goals are directly tied to our vision and mission.

    1   2   3   4   5

6. I take opportunities at least monthly to remind my employees of this organization's vision and mission.

    1   2   3   4   5

7. I have SMART goals for those employees who report to me.

    1   2   3   4   5

21

8. I regularly check my own work activities and projects to ensure they are focused and connected to the mission.

   1   2   3   4   5

9. I take opportunities to sharpen my vision on a regular basis.

   1   2   3   4   5

10. The vision is God-sized, so only He can receive the credit and glory when it is accomplished.

   1   2   3   4   5

11. The vision I (or our organization) have is not to serve me but is to serve the needs of others.

   1   2   3   4   5

12. When accomplished, the vision will have an eternal impact.

   1   2   3   4   5

13. We take active steps to ensure that our customers, suppliers and others in the community know our vision.

   1   2   3   4   5

14. I have a personal mission statement that defines my life purpose from an eternal perspective.

   1   2   3   4   5

15. Our employees clearly know what we do that differentiates us from our competition.

   1   2   3   4   5

16. Our organization has a clear picture of our target customers or a clear picture of our target market.

   1   2   3   4   5

17. We regularly seek customer feedback on our performance and assess that feedback against our stated mission and core values.

   1   2   3   4   5

18. We gracefully and lovingly encourage employees who do not agree with our vision to leave the organization.

1   2   3   4   5

19. We actively discuss our vision, mission and core values with applicants and try to gain their agreement of these before hiring them.

1   2   3   4   5

20. Our vision, mission and core values are aligned with biblical teachings.

1   2   3   4   5

Total your score here: _____

If you scored between 80 and 100 – Congratulations, you have set and are executing a vision with eternal impact.

If you scored between 60 and 79 – You have made some great progress, yet have a way to go before truly having a vision that has eternal impact.

If you scored under 60 – You are encouraged to take the necessary steps outlined in this chapter to develop a vision, mission and core values for you and/or your organization that will strive to have an eternal impact.

Practical Steps to Setting A Vision

As you read through and consider adopting some of these practices, take the opportunity to identify what you will eliminate from your current practice – if you need help in identifying what to eliminate, ask a trusted colleague, friend or advisor who is well versed in this critical aspect of leadership.

1. Examine the current vision, mission and core value statements for relevancy to today's conditions of the organization and the marketplace. Establish an advisory team to review and update these foundational documents, allowing the right amount of time for this exercise.
2. Examine the objectives and goals for you and your team to determine if they really connect to the vision and mission; alter as needed with involvement from your team and an outside advisor or facilitator if needed.
3. Respectfully challenge your colleagues if you sense the objectives or goals for their departments or divisions are not consistent with your understanding of the broader corporate or organization-wide vision and mission.
4. Reinforce to your staff that you expect them to hold you accountable to behave in alignment with the core values.
5. Ensure all goals are in the SMART format and are written.
6. Hold update sessions with your staff on their progress in meeting their goals at least on a quarterly basis, preferably on a monthly basis.
7. Prepare a personal vision and mission statement for you. Consider including your desire to hear, "Well done good and faithful servant" when you are welcomed home to heaven.
8. Develop a specific action plan to increase your assessment scores to the 80 – 100 range; ask others to hold you accountable and review your progress with them regularly.

9. Re-read the gospel accounts and note specifically where Jesus did the following: spoke or cast His vision; met opposition to His vision and His response to the opposition; and demonstrated an appreciation for His audience when speaking of His vision or purpose. Compare His actions to your actions and resolve to strive to be more like Christ.
10. Ensure your mission statement answers the five questions outlined in the discussion of that topic. Modify your mission statement accordingly.
11. Schedule quarterly meetings to review the vision, mission and core values with your staff.
12. If any of your staff is opposed to the vision or mission, develop and implement a plan to discuss their opposition with them or support them in exiting the organization.

CHAPTER TWO

QUIET TIME AND PRAYER

Leaders pray unceasingly

Scripture Passages

- "When I heard this, I sat down and wept. In fact, for days I mourned, fasted and prayed to the God of heaven." (Nehemiah 1:4 NLT)
- "Then you will call upon Me and go and pray to Me and I will listen to you. And you will seek Me and find Me, when you search for Me with all your heart (says the Lord)." (Jeremiah 29:12-13 NKJV)
- "One day soon afterward Jesus went up on a mountain to pray, and he prayed to God all night. At daybreak he called together all of his disciples and chose twelve of them to be apostles." (Luke 6:12-13 NLT)
- "They (the apostles) all met together and were constantly united in prayer..." (Acts 1:14 NLT)

Introduction

As busy leaders, many of us spend a great deal of time in our organizations taking care of the most pressing issues of the day or week. Our calendars are full of meetings, problem solving, and seeking and responding to opportunities. In strong growth or economic times, we are busy managing the growth and ensuring our customers or constituents are happy. In challenging economic times, we are busy trying to cut costs, preserve cash flow and go the extra mile to maintain market share and revenue.

When confronted with the challenging times, regardless of the challenge, some of us find time to seek the Lord in prayer and perhaps carve out occasional quiet time to read Scripture. We tend to seek the Lord when we, our organizations or our families are in trouble. We try to understand what is going on and what God wants us to do; we might even seek direction from godly people.

Do we really think that we can successfully perform our leadership responsibilities based on our own talents and abilities? Many of us only reach out for God when we are either humbled enough to realize we do not understand what is going on or we are humbled enough to accept that we cannot accomplish the challenge on our own. In the Leadership Development Survey conducted in Fall 2008, more than 30 percent of the almost 600 respondents said they were either "somewhat dissatisfied" or "very dissatisfied" with their relationship with God. Additionally, 30 percent expressed the same ratings when asked about their prayer and devotional time. Scripture tells us that regardless of our circumstances, the Lord desires a consistent relationship with each one of us. Knowing this, why do some of us only reach out during the challenging times?

This chapter will explore what Scripture tells us regarding having quiet time with our Lord and the role prayer has in our lives as leaders. We will discover that being more knowledgeable about the Scriptures is a worthy goal; that God wants a relationship with us all the time, not just in times of trouble. We will discover that if we spend daily time with God and we allow Him to speak to us, He will set our agenda for the day in a way that is so much more effective than we could possibly design on our own.

Henry Blackaby, a prominent Christian leader, tells the story of encouraging busy Fortune 500 CEOs to spend daily time with the Lord. He said that "spending unhurried time with God each morning is the greatest single time saver for a CEO as more can happen when the God of the universe instructs you in the beginning of the day than any other single thing." One of the CEOs responded by telling Henry that he did not realize how busy he was to which Henry replied, "You underestimate the significance of the Almighty God."

We are all busy. Consider, however, that we all have exactly 168 hours in a week. No one can add to or subtract from that number. We choose how we spend that time. Many of the more successful Christian leaders (as defined as having a Kingdom impact) will readily acknowledge they spend significant amounts of time in quiet time and prayer. Only those leaders with great discipline have a regular and consistent priority in devoting time to be quiet with the Lord, to seek and know Him through His Word and to pray. Let us learn what they know.

Biblical Foundation

Nehemiah demonstrated the importance of and reliance on prayer over and over again. In the first chapter of this biblical text, we learn that he wept, fasted, and prayed when told of the trouble his fellow Jews were in. Next, he prayed before he responded to King Artaxerxes' question of what Nehemiah wanted. As he and his fellow workers are rebuilding the wall and the various gates, we learn that after each job was completed, they dedicated it (3:1). Sometimes it seems the prayer was said before the work and at other times after the work was completed. We should interpret this as a lesson for us as leaders to pray before AND after a task.

When Nehemiah was sure he would face opposition he prayed, "Hear O our God, for we are despised." (4:4), and "Remember me, my God, for good, according to all that I have done for this people." (5:19 NKJV), and "Now therefore, O God, strengthen my hands." (6:9 NKJV) In chapter nine, more than thirty verses are recorded as a prayer of thanksgiving to God for His provision to the Jews throughout history and the confession of the sins committed by them and their forefathers.

The task Nehemiah was undertaking was without a doubt an enormous challenge. He needed material resources, he would face opposition, he needed encouragement and his followers would become tired. Nehemiah demonstrated for us that such a large undertaking can only be realized when prayer is a central part of the plan.

What can we learn from the various prayers he offers? First and foremost, he acknowledges the power of God and the love He has for His people. Nehemiah remembers aloud just how mighty and amazing his God really is on several occasions throughout this book. He speaks with reverence and respect as he describes God as "the great and awesome God who keeps his covenant of unfailing love with those who love him and obey his commands." (1:5 NLT) In chapter nine, God is described as "from everlasting to everlasting." *Prayer is for the people.*

We also observe that Nehemiah knew the Scriptures. In 1:8 (NLT) he said in his prayer to God, "Please remember what you told your servant Moses" and he quoted a passage from Leviticus and just a verse later, he quoted Deuteronomy. After the wall was built and Nehemiah was leading the people in the celebration, a key aspect of the celebration was to read what Moses had written, which was referred to as the Law. Ensuring that the people understood Scripture's importance as well as its teachings was a priority for Nehemiah.

Nehemiah also confessed his sins and the sins of his forefathers. He does this repeatedly as if to say that he is constantly aware of the faults, and that because of these faults, he has no right to come before his powerful and just God. He clearly acknowledged that neither he nor his forefathers have obeyed God's command or decrees. God wants us to be truthful

Relationship,

when we pray to Him. He certainly knows that we are not perfect, and He wants us to admit this to Him by being humble and honest about our faults.

Thirdly, Nehemiah made sure he thanked God for all the blessings he and the rest of the Jews had received. He was especially mindful of all that God had done through the years to protect and provide for the Jewish nation. Nehemiah acknowledged God's great compassion despite the Jews' regular disobedience of the laws and their desire to abandon their God when times were difficult.

Finally, Nehemiah asked for his needs to be met, whether for guidance, direction, wisdom, strength or protection. We have all heard many times how important it is to distinguish needs from wants when we go to the Lord in prayer. Nehemiah demonstrated this so well. *Relationship thru Needs*

This format of prayer is taught today as the ACTS model which is an acronym for Adoration, Confession, Thanksgiving and Supplication. This format will be discussed in more detail in the *Practical Application* section later in this chapter.

Jeremiah 29:12-13 reminds us that we must initiate prayer with a sincere heart. Jeremiah is writing these words from God in a letter to those Israelites who were taken captive by Nebuchadnezzar. These words are meant to be encouraging. They are also meant to communicate God's requirement for sincerity. Obviously, the people have been carried off because of their sin and God desired to gain their attention, but never to abandon them.

He told them to build their houses and families so the people would increase and not decrease. He commanded them to pray to the Lord for peace in the city where they now lived. Jeremiah, speaking for the Lord, says that when the captives "will call upon Me and go and pray to Me" that the Lord will listen to them. They will seek Him and find Him when they search with their heart; in other words, with sincerity. They must have right motives in seeking the Lord.

In this letter, Jeremiah was writing to the captives on behalf of the Lord. He told them they would have to wait some time (70 years) before they could expect improvement in their circumstances, yet he implored them to build their lives AND to continue to pray. He also warned them to watch for false prophets, for the Lord knew they would be influenced as captives to live lifestyles that were unpleasing to God. If the captives were regularly in prayer, it would be hard to adopt a lifestyle displeasing to God. It would be hard to begin worshiping idols. God has the same strategy in mind for us as leaders today – if we focus on praying it will help us to avoid the today's idols (focus on worry, money, fame, power, etc.). The Lord outlined His plans for the captives; all they had to do was to follow His requirements. *Relationship Reduced to Ritual!*

We find many examples of the Old Testament writers quoting from the first five books. The writers and the prophets were well versed in the Scripture. They would regularly reference it in their daily life. God must have had a good reason for these writers to emphasize this as much as they did. We can benefit from the lessons that are taught in these passages. Some of the key lessons include faith, courage, sincerity of heart, confession, fearing God and distinctions between being self reliant and reliant on God.

Another verse well worth considering is "Commit your actions to the Lord and your plans will succeed" (Proverbs 16:3 NLT). We commit by praying first. If we seek the Lord's will for our lives and our organizations and if we are truly focused on living out His will and not ours, then our plans will succeed.

If anyone did not need prayer, it was Jesus. Yet how often in the gospels do we read of Jesus praying? Jesus demonstrated that prayer must be a central part of our lives. Jesus, who knew all things and knew how all events would actually unfold, prayed regularly. He prayed out of respect for the Father. He prayed in thanksgiving on many occasions, and He went alone to pray and to spend time with His Father. Jesus taught us the Lord's Prayer and the necessity of faith.

In Luke 6, Jesus spent the night in prayer and in the morning appointed the 12 apostles. Do you think the selection of these men was part of His prayer time with the Father? We do not know for sure, but we are certainly led to believe this is the case. Of course, Jesus knew that Judas would betray Him;

perhaps He was asking the Father for reassurance of the plan for what it would teach us years and centuries later. The obvious lesson is that as Christian leaders, we must devote considerable time to prayer before we make important decisions that will impact the organization we are leading.

Jesus knew the disciples who would be selected as apostles would each have to carry a load as a leader. He knew the actions of each one would have consequences that would be felt for centuries. He knew their character had to be strong enough to withstand the inevitable attacks that would come upon them. These men were the ones in whom He was going to leave His legacy. He had to make sure they were the correct choices. Do we as leaders consider the selection decisions we make as carefully and as prayerfully as Jesus modeled?

In John 17, Jesus modeled for us that as leaders we must pray for those who will take our place and for those who will take on major assignments. Jesus had spent more than three years with this inner circle of men. He trained them to take up the cause. One might think this was enough, yet Jesus prayed for them. He prayed for their protection. He prayed that they would be unified. He prayed that their activities going forward would successfully accomplish God's purposes. We must continually pray for those under our authority.

Jesus says that God will protect His own who cry out day and night to Him. We must demonstrate persistence when we pray. As leaders we must persistently pray for our business – our employees, our customers, our suppliers and yes, even our competitors.

Jesus knew the Scriptures well. Consider the time He spent in the desert prior to beginning His public ministry when He was tempted three times by the devil. He relied on Scripture to battle the devil's temptations. He had a Scriptural response and answer to each temptation. He modeled for us how knowing the Truth would set Him free from the temptations, even the strongest of temptations. When Jesus was 12, He stayed behind in Jerusalem after celebrating one of the feasts (see Luke 2). He was speaking with the religious teachers, listening to them and asking them questions. Although it is not explicitly stated, most would agree that Jesus was not discussing the weather or the market cost of animals used for sacrifices. He was most likely discussing their knowledge and interpretation of Scripture. After all, verse 47 said the teachers were amazed at His understanding.

Jesus also used His knowledge of the Scriptures frequently when correcting the Pharisees. In Matthew 15 Jesus rebuked the Pharisees and teachers for going against the commands of God, as told in Scripture, for the sake of their traditions. This was one of the many times He called them hypocrites. He then quoted from Isaiah; a clear demonstration of His Scriptural knowledge.

This knowledge was not only modeled by Jesus, but by Paul, Peter, James and John in their New Testament writings. In Acts, we have examples of both Phillip and Stephen quoting Scripture; Phillip to the Ethiopian Treasurer and Stephen to the Jewish council. Key leaders of the day relied on very well developed knowledge of the Scripture. If common and uneducated people relied on Scripture so much, we should take notice of this pattern also. Remember, these leaders (with the exception of Paul) were not religious leaders; they were business people.

Another strong example of prayer is found in Acts 1 where we are told that the apostles "all joined together constantly in prayer, along with the women and Mary the mother of Jesus, and with His brothers" (Acts 1:14 NLT). The NKJV translation adds the words "and supplication" after prayer. So the apostles were all aligned in how they were praising God and asking for direction. After all, they had just witnessed Christ being taken up to heaven – not an everyday experience to say the least!

Prior to choosing a replacement for Judas, Luke tells us that they prayed in order that they would make the selection God had planned. Acts 1:24 (NKJV) says, "And they prayed and said, 'You, O Lord, who know the hearts of all, show which of these two You have chosen to take part in this ministry ...' " They knew not to rely on their own assessment of the candidates and they knew God had already made the choice. Their faithfulness through prayer revealed God's selection.

The next recorded time the apostles had to choose additional leaders is in Acts 6. It was brought to their attention that the Grecian widows were being neglected. They brought the other disciples together to discuss the problem. Notice they knew they should not divert from the work they were already doing in expanding the good news. They recognized that more appropriately equipped people should be appointed to effectively handle this problem. They knew their prime responsibility was to give themselves "continually to prayer and the ministry of the word." (Acts 6:4 NKJV) Notice also that after the seven were selected, they prayed over them. Prayer does not end when the decision is made. Prayer continues on to ensure the correct decision has been made and is implemented according to God's purposes. As previously discussed, Jesus modeled this for us in John 17.

Lessons Learned about Quiet Time and Prayer

1. One of the best leaders of the Bible, Nehemiah, prayed frequently. We as leaders should follow his example.
2. The motives for praying to God must be sincere and pure in heart.
3. Commit all major decisions to prayer before making the decision.
4. All key leaders in the Bible, most of who were business people, had an exceptionally strong foundational knowledge of Scripture. They had the Scriptural knowledge and foundation *before* God used them.

Practical Application

During the past couple of decades, Fortune 500 companies merged with or acquired other companies to become larger and larger. Many of these companies used the rationale that they could generate more revenue and profits if they served a larger portion of the marketplace or combined redundant departments. Obviously, this strategy in and of itself is not necessarily a poor or evil strategy. By acquiring or expanding, these merged organizations could take financial advantage of the synergies formed by becoming larger. We all know what some of those promised synergies are: increased customer base, improved efficiency in manufacturing or services, and additional capital to invest in future growth.

We know the end of the story for many of these organizations. They would eventually lay off thousands of workers because they were not meeting the financial targets they set to achieve. These layoffs were after the initial "right-sizing" layoffs to reduce duplicate functions. Some of these companies did not survive. Many of you might have been impacted in one way or another by the "merger-mania" that has taken place. The impact to you might have come in the form of changes in your position, career or other job opportunities, or the impact might have come from your experience as a consumer of, or supplier to, the "new and improved" products or services the bigger organization had to offer. While not all mergers have failed, many have not been entirely successful.

Would it surprise you to learn that most of these acquisitions and mergers were not considered successful especially when measured against the criteria originally established for the merger or acquisition in the first place? In fact, using the stock price as one measure, as you study the stock performance of the mergers, the vast majority will show a lower price as compared to the price prior to the merger. There are many reasons for these failures and those reasons are the subject of other articles and books. One of the prime reasons for these failures is hardly mentioned in these books at all. One of the prime reasons might not be the failure to plan effectively, but it could very possibly be the consequences of failing to ask the Lord for direction and wisdom prior to initiating the plans.

Proverbs 19:21 (NLT) says, "You can make many plans, but the Lord's purposes will prevail." And 20:18 (NLT) says, "Plans succeed through good counsel; don't go to war without wise advice." Today, we interpret war as doing the business of our organization. The proverb is advising us to seek godly counsel before making major decisions such as mergers, acquisitions, expansions and the like. As Christians, we know the Lord's plans will not be thwarted. Yet, we as humans regularly challenge His plan, and many of us wonder why we were not successful in the execution of those plans.

One of King David's good traits was that he regularly (although not always) relied on God for guidance. Before going into battles (see I Samuel 30:7-9), David would seek God. This character trait is common among some of the greatest biblical leaders including Moses, Samuel, Deborah, Gideon and Joshua. Proverbs 16:9 says that man makes his plans but the Lord directs his steps. We must be keenly aware if our plans are not working out that God very possibly is re-directing our steps to be in His will.

There are many examples in Scripture when leaders did not seek guidance from God (or, worse yet, refused to heed His guidance), and the result was evil or horrific. The message is

37

clear: seek God's guidance and patiently wait on His direction. He is Sovereign in all things, including timing. His work is never late, never early; it is always perfect.

Scripture clearly states that God wants to be part of our planning for all aspects of our lives. Proverbs 16:3 (NLT) says it all, "Commit your actions to the Lord and your plans will succeed." Somehow, we have learned to put this practice in reverse order. A very simple analogy is that we treat our prayer requests to God similarly as we would if we were in a restaurant. Sometimes, we "place our order" to God for what we desire to have or think we need to address our hunger situation. Our flawed tendency can be to plan first then pray that the Lord will bless our plans. This verse clearly tells us to pray first and make plans second according to the insight we receive during our prayer.

Please do not misunderstand, the Bible is certainly not against organizational growth. Look at the growth of the Church! Some of the best organizations in the world today have achieved their success by employing such growth strategies. Prayer is a central and required ingredient to such growth, assuming that growth is within the Lord's sovereign plan for that organization.

Many godly leaders talk about how important their prayer life is to them. In fact, many begin and end each day by reading Scripture and meditate on the Word throughout the day. Many say that their day is just not right when they forget or otherwise omit prayer on a particular day. Some have said that they rely on their morning prayer time to help set their goals and priorities for the day. They have faith that God will direct them where they need to spend their time. This can only occur when the day begins with quiet time, alone with Him.

It is important for us to pray not just when we need something, but regularly throughout the day in all circumstances. Praying in thanksgiving is just as glorifying to God as praying for Him to provide for our needs. We are called to pray for others. Paul provides us with an example in many of his letters. He tells us how he remembers those he is writing to with statements such as "in all my prayers for all of you" (Philippians 1:4); "We always thank God for all of you and pray for you constantly." (I Thessalonians 1:2 NLT)

Prayer is God's gift for us to be in communication with Him. How wonderful it is that we do not have to be in a special place, use a special introductory code, or perform some ritualistic act to initiate prayer! All we have to do is start a private conversation with God. We have a direct connection to the One who knows our needs best and who provides us with unconditional love. Paul commands us to use prayer when he advises the Philippians, "Do not be anxious about anything, but in everything, by prayer and petition, with thanksgiving, present your requests to God." (Philippians 4:6)

With little or no prayer, leaders might make popular, pleasant, intelligent and captivating decisions that result in some good or benefit. But the leadership that comes from God's leading must be born of prayer from the beginning to the completion of a task, assignment, strategy or initiative.

The little regard we give quiet time and prayer is evident from the little time we spend in prayer. With only 168 hours in a week, how much is spent in understanding the Scriptures and in prayer? If we say that God is our first priority then is it not reasonable to dedicate a significant amount of our time to Him in prayer and in understanding His will?

Psalm 78 recounts the history of the Israelites rebellion against God despite the many occasions He provided deliverance, protection and basic sustenance. There are many parallels of this psalm to our life as leaders in the world today. By media, marketing and self-centered standards, we are rebelling against God and forgetting all the blessings and provision He has given us. We must spend more time in His Word and with Him and far less time in the media and culture of today so we do not continue in this rebellion and forget any more of what God has so graciously provided.

NewSpring Church pastor, Perry Noble, said, "Effective prayer is when I begin to focus on what God wants to do in me, around me, through me and for me." We need to ask God to show us the purpose He has for us and why He made us. We need to ask God to teach us to see as He sees and to clearly tell us the next steps we are to take in all aspects of our lives, including those as Christian leaders.

The ACTS (Adoration, Confession, Thanksgiving and Supplication) model of prayer was referenced earlier. This is an effective way to pray in part because we consciously take the focus off us and rightfully place it on God. When we spend the initial time in Adoration of our Holy God, Lord and Savior, we are praising His name and His attributes; telling of our love for Him. Reflecting on certain verses in psalms or current day hymns that magnify His name is one way to express your adoration. Reflecting on His names and His attributes are other ways to express your adoration. If we were to truly focus on all His attributes, this alone could take hours.

Taking time to Confess our sins is an important aspect of prayer. Romans 3:23 says that we have all sinned and fall short of God's standards. This is a statement that is always accurate. We all fall short, and we all sin – all the time. When we accept that even the most humble and God-fearing among us have occasion to sin, having the opportunity to confess that sin in our alone time with our heavenly Father is an awesome privilege. This is the time we can also show true repentance for our sin and ask for His help in protecting us from falling into that sin or temptation in the future.

The next aspect is to be Thankful for what God has provided. This is a good time to reflect on the gifts, resources, talents, events, and opportunities that God has allowed us to experience. This is a good time to thankfully reflect on decisions that God has made possible. It is also a good time to thank Him for what He has been doing in your life and other's lives. It is a good time to thank Him for healing others and for protecting you from things you were not aware of that would have been harmful to you. We can never take for granted what God has done for us, what He is doing for us and what He will do for us.

The last aspect is Supplication or asking for Him to provide for our needs and the needs of others. Matthew 6:31-32 (NLT) says, "So don't worry about these things, saying, 'What will we eat? What will we drink? What will we wear?' These things dominate the thoughts of unbelievers, but your heavenly

Father already knows all your needs." Is Jesus instructing us to not ask for our needs? No! He is commanding us to not worry about our needs because our heavenly Father already knows them in detail. Verse 33 goes on to say, "Seek the Kingdom of God above all else…"

As we pray, we are to seek the Kingdom of God first. We are to pray for His will to be done and not our own will. Jesus modeled this in His fervent prayer in the Garden the night before He was crucified. As Christian leaders, we are to pray for God's will to be done in regard to the organizational and life decisions we are pondering. We are to ask for His will to be done in the employee selection decisions we are making. We are to ask for His will to be done when praying for the burdens of others.

Jesus promises us that if we seek His kingdom first, all of our needs will be met. By mentioning the unbelievers in verse 32, Jesus wants us to be distinguished from them by our prayer life. He desires for Christians to be set apart from unbelievers and for our behavior to be noticeably different from their behavior even in our prayer life.

Prayer should not be a repetitive pattern of the same words over and over. This approach will lead to an insincere prayer life. The ACTS model is an effective way to order your time alone with God and to ensure you are focusing on the items that will bring you closer to Him.

Scripture is so powerful in providing key lessons about all areas of life, from forgiveness to handling money to relating with people. The Bible is really an Operations Manual for life, and it has many lessons for leaders. It suggests and sometimes commands how we must behave. It clearly tells us the expectations God has for us.

We must commit time to understand all of what the Bible has to say. This could very well be an overwhelming task, especially for someone who is not "in ministry." However, if you agree the Bible has many important lessons for us to learn why not spend more time trying to uncover those lessons? According to Dave Rae, as he narrates the Business By The Book Workshop, most businesses that were in operation in the 1800s and early 1900s operated their companies using biblical principles. Why have businesses today shifted away from this approach? The reasons are beyond the scope of this book other than to say that greed, pride, selfishness and other similar destructive elements are likely the cause.

Proverbs is filled with wise advice about many of life's issues and concerns. It provides advice on leadership, how to treat other people, key trouble areas to avoid, habits to avoid as well as habits to develop and many other insights. Many people find it helpful to read a chapter of Proverbs each day. In one month, you will have read the entire book. Steven Scott, in his book, *The Richest Man Who Ever Lived*, talks about Solomon's secrets to success, wealth and happiness. He suggests reading through the book of Proverbs one chapter per day each month for two years. He also suggests noting key topical areas that Proverbs addresses and writing the specific proverbs that relate to that topical area.

Charles Sheldon, in his book, *In His Steps*, tells the story of a Midwest pastor who challenged his congregation by asking for volunteers who would "pledge themselves earnestly and honestly for an entire year not to attempt anything without first asking the question, 'What would Jesus do?'" The book describes how life changing this commitment was not just to the people, including some business leaders, who accepted the challenge but to the entire community who were recipients of the volunteer's actions.

Needless to say these volunteers could not have lived their lives asking the question 'What would Jesus do?' if they did not commit to know how Jesus taught His disciples. This required a strong knowledge of the gospels and other Scripture. As committed Christians we must have an equally strong desire to know the Scriptures.

Noted Bible teacher, Chuck Swindoll, has commented on the lack of biblical knowledge in our society. He says that "our thinking is no longer based on the objective truth of the Bible." This is quite alarming – even scary. If our thinking is not based on the truth of the Bible, it must be based on the widely popular trends of the secular society. This is dangerous to say the least.

We must alter this course, and it has to begin with us. After all, as Christian leaders, we have influence over others.

A wise habit to develop is to have a part of each day devoted to reading, studying and mediating on Scripture and to pray. For many people, the first part of the day is the most appropriate time so they can hear what God has planned for them before they move on with the business or busyness of the day. Another wise habit is to have a Scripture reading plan. Many are available and can be obtained from your church, Christian bookstore or online.

Additionally, take extra time each month or each quarter for more extensive reading, study, meditation and prayer. Taking such time prior to major organizational planning sessions or discussions will be time well spent. Knowing that you are aligned with God's will for your life and your organization is a goal to strive for, and it can only happen if you take sufficient time to be in God's word and prayer. Henry Blackaby refers to this as "unhurried time" alone with God.

As a Christian leader it is helpful to join and participate in a Christian leader's ministry such as Fellowship of Companies for Christ International (www.fcci.org), C12 Group (www.C12Group.com) or similar organization. The purpose of these ministries to equip and encourage business leaders to run their organizations and lives using biblical principles. They generally provide resources and have meetings with other Christian leaders who are looking for such equipping and mutual encouragement.

Consider reading books that will expand your knowledge and application of Scripture. While traveling in your car or on a plane, play messages from some well-known Bible teachers (you can download from the Internet) and keep a journal of the insights you obtain. Discuss these insights with other members of your equipping group, your spouse or other people who will help deepen your understanding even further.

We are clearly called to know Scripture. All the great leaders of the Bible knew Scripture. Even great leaders before the 20th century knew the Scripture. They quoted it often. As Christian leaders, will you commit to having quiet time and prayer time with the Lord? As Paul said in Romans 12:2 (NLT), "Don't copy the behaviors and customs of this world, but let God transform you into a new person by changing the way you think. Then you will learn to know God's will for you, which is good and pleasing and perfect." The way we can be transformed is by knowing His Word more thoroughly, and this will change the way we think. Proverbs 2:12 (NLT) says that wisdom, which is provided by God through His Word "will save you from evil people, from those whose words are twisted." Today, more than any other time in history, we need to follow and obey these commands.

Proverbs 9:10 says, "The fear of the Lord is the beginning of wisdom, and knowledge of the Holy One is understanding." This verse or a similar verse is repeated several times in Scripture. To fear the Lord, one has to know a lot about Him. This can only happen by spending time in His Word and in prayer. When we spend this committed and unhurried time, we gain knowledge of the Holy One. With knowledge of the Holy One comes understanding. When we fill ourselves with this knowledge, other worldly sources of knowledge and falsehood will be pushed out of our minds. They will be exposed for what they are – false and unreliable. The more exposure we have to God through His Word, to His ways, to His promises and to His character, the more we will be in awe of Him and have an awesome relationship with Him. This is true fear of the Lord and it is the beginning of wisdom – wisdom for our lives, wisdom for our families, wisdom for our careers and wisdom for our roles as Christian leaders.

In Romans 16:17-18 (NLT), Paul gives a final warning to the Romans when he cautions them to "watch out for people who cause divisions and upset people's faith by teaching things contrary to what you have been taught. Stay away from them. Such people are not serving Christ our Lord; they are serving their own personal interests. By smooth talk and glowing words they deceive innocent people." The focus here is to stick to how God's Word instructs us in living our lives and being a Christian leader. This passage also tells us to be aware of false teachings by others whose interests are self-centered and not God-centered. We must be careful to not be fooled into being self-seeking rather than God-seeking in our quiet time and prayer. We must be careful as to the sources of advice, wisdom and guidance we rely on to help us make decisions. We maximize our ability to follow Paul's command when we have unhurried quiet time and prayer on a daily basis.

Self Assessment

Below are twenty statements that are indicative of behaviors of those who are committed to quiet time and prayer. As you read these statements, be aware of the first response that comes to mind as it related to your quiet time and prayer life and circle the number in the appropriate column.

Never – 1	Seldom – 2	Sometimes – 3	Usually – 4	Always – 5

1. I read Scripture daily.

        1   2   3   4   5

2. I utilize a plan to read Scripture. I do not haphazardly open up Scripture and read any passage.

        1   2   3   4   5

3. I have daily time alone with God in prayer.

        1   2   3   4   5

4. I regularly pray with my spouse or other prayer partner.

        1   2   3   4   5

5. I regularly discuss what I have learned in Scripture with someone else.

        1   2   3   4   5

6. I pray to understand God's will and direction before making important decisions.

        1   2   3   4   5

7. I pray for God's will and not mine to be done.

        1   2   3   4   5

8. I use prayer time to confess my sins and my other transgressions.

        1   2   3   4   5

Quiet Time And Prayer

9. I use prayer time to thank God for all the wonderful blessings He has bestowed on me.

       1   2   3   4   5

10. I record insights I obtain from reading Scripture in a journal.

       1   2   3   4   5

11. I regularly listen to messages from well-known Bible teachers to grow my knowledge of the Scriptures.

       1   2   3   4   5

12. I belong to a Christian leader fellowship group and regularly attend and share at their meetings.

       1   2   3   4   5

13. My schedule reflects proper balance between God and work.

       1   2   3   4   5

14. I have clarity on the biblical values that guide my decision making.

       1   2   3   4   5

15. I regularly pray for others including staff, customers, suppliers and competitors.

       1   2   3   4   5

16. I read books to edify my knowledge and application of Scripture.

       1   2   3   4   5

17. I offer to pray with and for my employees and colleagues.

       1   2   3   4   5

18. I regularly assess how I can use my time more effectively in knowing God better.

       1   2   3   4   5

19. The place I go to read God's word and pray is void of distractions and interruptions.

1   2   3   4   5

20. I regularly take time to meditate on a specific verse for application to my life as a leader.

1   2   3   4   5

Total your score here: _____

If you scored between 80 and 100 – Congratulations, you are well on your way to having a strong quiet time and prayer life.

If you scored between 60 and 79 – You have made some great progress, yet have a way to go before truly having a strong quiet time and prayer life.

If you scored under 60 – You are encouraged to examine your quiet time and prayer behaviors and eliminate those that are not contributing to a strong quiet time and prayer life.

Practical Steps to Exhibit Quiet Time and Prayer

As you read through and consider adopting some of these practices, take the opportunity to identify what you will eliminate from your current practice – if you need help in identifying what to eliminate, ask a trusted colleague, friend or advisor.

1. Set aside time each day, ideally the same time each day, to devote to quiet time and prayer.
2. As you set aside time to be alone with God each day, listen for what He wants to tell you rather than asking for His blessing on plans you have already decided.
3. In your daily prayer time, ask God to clearly establish your agenda for the day so you can focus on what He desires for you to accomplish.
4. Identify specific objectives you desire in spending more time in quiet time and prayer.
5. Regularly check your motives to ensure they are sincere and pure in heart for God's purposes and not about your plans or desires.
6. Commit to pray with your spouse or other prayer partner at set times each week.
7. As you read Scripture, use a journal to record some key insights that come to mind as you read particular verses, chapters or books of the Bible.
8. Allow sufficient time for prayer before committing to major organizational decisions. Ensure you know how God is leading you before such decisions are made.
9. Become an active participant in a Christian leader fellowship group that provides opportunities for you to pray for and with fellow members.
10. Develop a plan and a behavior to regularly listen to messages from well-known Bible teachers such as Chuck Swindoll, Chip Ingram, Henry Blackaby and others who will build your knowledge of the Scriptures.
11. Develop an annual book-reading plan that includes a book per month from a well-known Bible teacher.

12. Establish a group that will commit to join you in steps 10 and 11 and be willing to discuss insights received on a monthly basis.
13. Ensure your schedule reflects an appropriate balance in spending quiet time with God and your other activities, including work demands.
14. Ask each of your employees or colleagues how you can pray for them on a weekly basis.
15. Remember to pray for your customers, suppliers and even your competitors on a regular basis.
16. Identify a verse each week to meditate on and keep a journal where you can record your thoughts on that verse.
17. Consider adopting the ACTS model of prayer.
18. Commit to read the Bible in a year following a particular plan. Blackaby Ministries and Walk Thru The Bible are two of several organizations that have the Bible readings organized daily to complete the Bible in a year.
19. Ensure you have a small council of godly advisors whose wisdom you can seek before any major decision is made, regardless of your leadership role.
20. Commit to read a chapter of Proverbs each day for a year and maintain a journal with the insights and advice you will receive.
21. Start a prayer list in your department or organization, and ask others to contribute their prayer requests. Commit as a group to pray for those requests on a weekly basis in a group prayer setting.
22. Spend time before going to bed to reflect on how God worked in your life that day, thanking Him for His work and listening for His feedback.

CHAPTER THREE

SERVANT LEADERSHIP

Are you serving self or others?

Scripture Passages

- "Don't be selfish; don't try to impress others. Be humble, thinking of others as better than yourselves. Don't look out only for your own interests, but take an interest in others, too." (Philippians 2:3-4 NLT)
- "You know that the rulers in this world lord it over their people, and officials flaunt their authority over those under them. But among you it will be different. Whoever wants to be a leader among you must be your servant, and whoever wants to be first among you must become your slave. For even the Son of Man came not to be served but to serve others and to give his life as a ransom for many." (Matthew 20:25-28 NLT)
- "Care for the flock that God has entrusted to you. Watch it willingly, not grudgingly – not for what you will get out of it, but because you are eager to serve God. Don't lord it over the people assigned to your care, but lead them by your own good example." (I Peter 5:2-3 NLT)
- "The older counselors replied, 'If you are willing to be a servant to these people today and give them a favorable answer, they will always be your loyal subjects.' " (I Kings 12:7 NLT)

Introduction

The world is full of examples of leaders behaving in ways that disappoint many of the people they are impacting – whether it be their employees, shareholders, families, customers or suppliers. Open a newspaper, magazine or internet news source, and you will find no shortage of stories of leaders once trusted to influence and act on behalf of others who have seemingly gone off the deep end. Why is that? The answer might lie in understanding the focus of their motivation. Their motivation seems to be focused on self and not on others. Arguably, many of today's high profile leaders in both secular and Christian organizations have reached their position because they focused on self from either a perspective of pride or a perspective of fear. The root motivation of many of their leadership actions is based on protecting themselves rather than those they are leading.

We can find many examples of leaders who are using the status of their position to exploit employees, shareowners, customers or suppliers. Some make great attempts to insulate themselves from having to follow the rules. Unfortunately, there are almost countless public leaders who have been caught in lies, deceit and other behavior simply because they did not want to take full ownership or accountability of a situation or did not want to tarnish their reputation by admitting to a mistake. They did not want to face the scrutiny of the media for a mistake or misjudgment so they lied about facts, omitted important information or claimed it was someone else's responsibility.

The well-known author, John Maxwell, says, "everything rises and falls on leadership." He has also said, "leadership is about influence, nothing more and nothing less." Leaders earn the right to influence when they can be trusted to act for the best interests of the other person or organization. Therefore, effective leadership is "other" focused and not "self" focused. Unfortunately today, there are too many leaders who have gone to the "dark side" and are focused on self and not on others.

We can divide leadership styles into two camps – a "self-serving" leader vs. a "serving others" leader or a "power" leader vs. a "servant" leader. Serving or servant leaders care about others as much as, if not more than, themselves and show this by taking the time and effort to build real, transparent and trusting relationships with those they lead. Servant leaders also demonstrate genuine care for those who hold them accountable to lead – stakeholders, employees, customers and suppliers.

Power leaders on the other hand have more interest in their own needs and desires. At their worst, they see those they lead as there to serve them in their quest to gain as much power, control, prestige and recognition as possible. As Christian leaders, we are called to be servant leaders and not power leaders.

Biblical Foundation

Servant leadership has become a popular discussion topic in management and leadership books these days, but what is this all about, and how did it come to be?

The apostle Paul was certainly a servant leader. He visited and served the spiritual needs of his constituents by placing himself in great physical danger. He provided a significant example for his constituents to model. In Philippians, Paul described some of the traits of a leader who serves when he was describing Timothy. In Philippians 2:4-5 (NLT), Paul writes, "Don't be selfish; don't try to impress others. Be humble, thinking of others as better than yourselves. Don't look out only for your own interests, but take an interest in others, too." He goes on to describe how Jesus "made himself nothing taking the very nature of a servant … he humbled himself."

In describing some of the traits of Timothy, Paul said no one else took a genuine interest in the Philippians' welfare while pointing out that all others looked out for their own interests and not those of Jesus. Paul is giving us some of the traits of a servant leader. Some of these key traits include humility necessary to subordinate their own needs for the needs of others and taking the active step of looking out for the interests of other people. It is certainly hard to look out for the needs of others when we are more focused on our own needs. The Bible commands us as leaders to serve others.

Jesus practiced this kind of servant leadership and began a movement that has shaped the world for the last 2,000 years. In the first few months of the church, 5,000 men were saved and joined the Jerusalem church and Jesus was not there (physically)! What Jesus modeled as servant leadership is nothing less than the most effective leadership technique and style the world has ever known. Not only has His organization lasted longer than any other organization, He has in excess of two billion followers. It is pretty clear that Jesus' methods should be studied and modeled.

Jesus said, "Whoever wants to become great among you must be your servant." These are certainly some pretty strong words. Many people back in His days on earth as well as many of us today would view this statement as a contradiction.

At first glance, it might seem as though Jesus says some puzzling things, and this certainly ranks high on that list: *Someone great must be a servant.* But we say, "Great" people do not serve; people serve them. They have assistants, limousine drivers, agents, body guards and trailing reporters. So what was Jesus talking about? Very simply, He is talking about being of service to others first. He is telling us that we must look out for the needs of others.

The very act of Jesus coming to this earth shows that first and foremost He was a servant to His Father. That was His purpose and response in coming to earth – to serve His Father. As He engaged with people on earth, His ministry to those people came directly out of His calling to serve God the Father. His purpose was to fulfill the Father's desire in advancing the Kingdom and providing a way for humankind to be reconciled to the Father.

Jesus said, "The Son of Man did not come to be served, but to serve and to give His life." We are provided no wiggle room in the original language either. The Greek words translated *servant, served* and *serve* mean *to render assistance or help by performing certain duties, often of a humble or menial nature.* To make sure the point is clear, Jesus repeats His thought using the unmistakable word *slave*, someone owned by and therefore under the total control of another. He then demonstrates His point of performing menial tasks by washing the disciple's feet, a task usually reserved for slaves.

The Lord of heaven and earth serves His disciples as a slave? The Lord who owns the earth and everything in it (Psalm 24:1) came to serve others as a slave? Yes. Should we then serve those who are under our authority? Yes.

As John's gospel passage recounts, when Jesus approaches Peter to wash his feet, Peter implies that Jesus, as his Lord, should not perform the lowly task of washing his feet. Jesus replies "unless I wash you, you have no part with me." Then Peter replied, "not just my feet, but my hands and my head as well." Jesus provided ample motivation for Peter with a few simple words and Peter responded so emphatically and with such enthusiasm. Peter had accepted the notion that Jesus had earned the right to be the leader because of His service to Peter and others.

This might have been the turning point for Peter from being an ordinary leader to a servant leader. Later on we will discuss how Peter became a servant leader. It took him awhile, as it might take us; yet he provides a strong example of how people and their style can change if we are in a relationship with Jesus and submit daily to His authority.

Do not miss what John tells us just before Jesus went to wash the feet of the disciples. In John 13:3 (NLT) he writes, "Jesus knew that the Father had given him authority over everything and that he had come from God and would return to God." Then verse 4 begins the example of servant leadership. The motivation and attitude to be a servant leader comes from knowing your place with God. Jesus knew His place was as a servant to the Father. As Christians, we can be secure in operating as a servant leader since we are children of God, we are secure in our salvation, we commit to serve Jesus, and we bring glory and honor to Him in all we do. In verse 17, after the washing and the explanation by Jesus, He says, "Now that you know these things, God will bless you for doing them." Knowing that we are secure in our place as Christian leaders allows us to behave in a manner that He requires us to, even though this manner is against what the world expects, demands or sometimes even tolerates.

Here are some other ways that Jesus modeled servant leadership for us:

- He was never self-serving – He was always serving others or His Father (see John 6:38)
- He defined His greatness in being a leader as a servant (see Matthew 20:28).
- He humbled Himself to give up the position of authority at the Father's right hand to become a human who would suffer and die (see Philippians 2:6-7)
- He was confident in His position and could risk being a servant (see John 13:3). He knew where His authority came from.
- He taught and mentored those who would carry out a mission (see Luke 10:1-17).
- He served those who were most needy (see Mark 2:17).
- He was fully honest with those He led while training them (see Luke 10:3).

Nehemiah is generally looked upon as a leader with vision, as previously discussed in the *Setting a Vision* chapter. However, a closer look reveals that he was also a servant leader. Consider these verses of Nehemiah:

- In 1:3-4, his heart was broken; he was moved by the events that had happened in Jerusalem.
- In 2:1-5, we see that he went from the security of a job in the King's residence (albeit a sometimes dangerous job as the cupbearer) to be a leader who served others and was willing to put himself in great danger.
- In 2:11-18, we see that he personally assessed the situation rather than delegate it to one of his underlings, and he then took ownership of the situation and enlisted others to help.

- In 4:14, we see that he motivated his followers by having them work on the part of the wall that was near their own home and family.

Nehemiah was deeply moved by the situation and committed to do something about it. He not only saw the situation as a problem for the people who were fellow Jews, he saw the situation as negatively impacting the reputation of God. After all, this could be used by those who did not follow God to mock the way God protected His people. This might have been his motivation to jump to action and lead – to protect the reputation of God. Servant leaders see a need to serve others, not themselves.

We see that he looked out for the interests of others. He answered the call to lead. He saw the need to lead others as more important than continuing his regular day job for which he was highly regarded by the King. He was willing to give all that up to help and serve others who were in dire need of a leader. He knew there would be significant risks in making this move, yet he willingly sacrificed his pleasure and comfort in order to serve others he knew were important to God.

Nehemiah did not seek the position for fame, fortune or power. Rather, he saw a need, developed a passion to address the need and did whatever it took to respond to the need. He did not rush into this plan either; he took four months to pray, plan and determine the right timing to approach the King to ask permission for his leave of absence.

He did not use fear, insult or manipulation as his enemy did. Instead, he motivated his fellow workers by understanding their strengths and abilities and assigning work that was in line with those strengths and abilities. He motivated his workers by assigning them to work on areas near their homes. When others use fear, insult or manipulation, the temptation is to copy those techniques because they seem to be effective in getting people to move. Nehemiah did not succumb to this temptation. He maintained his original plan and motivated the people by his ability to influence and make the overall goal personal to them.

Let's now examine the transformation of Peter as a servant leader. At the end of John's gospel, we pick up the account when Jesus has been resurrected for several days. Peter and several other disciples have returned to the Sea of Galilee, and Peter decided to go fishing. They were out all night and had not caught a single fish. Jesus comes by in the early morning and calls out to them, "Throw out your net on the right-hand side of the boat and you'll catch some (fish)" (20:6 NLT). This time, Peter does not question Jesus as he did three years earlier. During those three years, and even after that, he was on a continual learning curve in understanding what it would take to become a servant leader.

After bringing the fish to shore, Jesus invites Peter and the others to have some breakfast. Here we are about to have the final interaction between Jesus and Peter while Jesus was on the earth. Jesus calls Peter into a life of servant leadership with the words, "Feed my lambs and feed my sheep." The act of feeding is obviously a serving mode, not a power mode. Do not miss this point – Jesus wanted to be sure that Peter knew that he loved Jesus above all else. With this motivation, then Jesus could ask Peter to be a servant to the mission and cause that Jesus came to establish – His Church.

Peter had more to learn, however. He then sees John and asks Jesus about him. Jesus kindly rebukes him and says, "What is that to you? As for you, follow me." Jesus was telling Peter not to be concerned about how others were going to lead – only be concerned and only focus on doing what He was asking, which was to feed His lambs and sheep. Jesus wanted Peter to make sure he stuck to the mission that Jesus gave him without concern for how other leaders would carry out the mission Jesus gave them. Does this sound familiar? How often do we become concerned about what our peer leaders are doing, rather than placing our full focus on what we are supposed to do as leaders?

As we continue to read about Peter in Acts, we start to appreciate that Peter is undergoing a process of transformation of his leadership style. He is no longer seeking to influence others for his gain; rather, he is following what Jesus asked him to do by feeding the lambs – the early church. Peter's words to others are all about glorifying God and Jesus, he is not testifying about his own skill and talent as a fisherman.

The first miracle performed by Peter was an act of service. He commands a crippled man who is sitting outside the temple begging for money to "get up and walk." What was the result? The man got up with strengthened feet and ankles, and he praised God. That is servant leadership and giving the glory to God. Christian servant leaders do this routinely because they know that it is not them working their talents but God working through them to accomplish His purposes. Peter also gives credit to God when other people came out to see what had happened to the crippled man. Because Peter gave God the credit, he was allowed to speak to the other people to influence them.

By allowing God to work through him, and by giving God the glory, this servant leader was following what Jesus had instructed him to do – feed his lambs. As a result, the church quickly grew from 120 to more than 5,000 (see Acts 4). That is how to influence others by being a servant to them. When people perceive that you care about them enough to serve them, they become more open to hearing what you have to say. This opens the door for us to talk about Jesus.

As a servant leader, Peter also demonstrated that he could still learn. Consider the account in Acts 10 where Peter sees the vision of all sorts of animals on a sheet. When God commands him to kill and eat the animals, Peter says he has never eaten anything that was unclean. God then responds by telling Peter to not call something God had made unclean. To say that this rocked Peter's world is an understatement. This was God's way of telling Peter that Gentiles, previously viewed as unclean, were now "eligible" to be part of God's family. What a learning experience for Peter! Servant leaders need to be open to learn new things all the time.

As we look at some of Peter's writings, it becomes clear that his transformation into a servant leader has become complete. In the first chapter of I Peter (NLT), he uses phrases such as "exercise self control," "don't slip back into your old ways of living to satisfy your own desires," "now you must be holy in everything you do," "you must live in reverent fear of (God)," "so now you must show sincere love to each other as brothers and sisters. Love each other deeply with all your heart." In the fifth chapter, he clearly directs elders (leaders) to "Care for the flock that God has entrusted to you. Watch over it willingly, not grudgingly – not for what you will get out of it, but because you are eager to serve God. Don't lord it over the people assigned to your care, but lead them by your own good example." (1 Peter 5:2-3 NLT) These are qualities of a servant leader, not a power leader.

Servant leaders also act with integrity. Servant leaders do what they say they are going to do. They consistently act the way they have committed to act. Once again, there is no better example than Jesus. The gospels have several examples of Jesus stopping what He was doing to be of service to others. His mission was to be a servant to His Father by doing the will of the Father, and the method He chose to use was by being of service to others.

As usual, the Word of God can provide us with examples of how to do something, as well as examples of how not to do something. The Bible has several examples of leaders who do not demonstrate the principle of servant leadership. In Matthew 2, we read about Herod's reaction to the birth of Jesus. He was a leader who was focused on himself and was worried that his position would be compromised if another 'king' was on the scene. Another king might threaten Herod's comfortable lifestyle and regal position among the people.

Herod was not about to meet others' needs by worshiping the new king. He was more concerned about his own needs and wanted to eliminate any competition or threat to his position. He was not truthful in his intentions (see Matthew 2:8). He was greedy and self serving. He let his anger rule his actions. Herod was a power leader – a leader who was very focused on himself.

Herod also taught these leadership "methods" to his son. In Matthew 14:3-5 we read how Herod junior exercised his power by jailing the people whose opinions disagreed with his.

We also read just a few verses later that he was so consumed with himself, he threw a lavish party for himself and invited only those who would heap praise on him and entertain him. This is a leader who clearly was more concerned about his own elevation than providing service to those under his authority.

Another negative example is demonstrated in the life of Rehoboam, found in I Kings 12. You might be familiar with the account of Solomon's son who was named king after Solomon died. Rehoboam blew an opportunity to establish a relationship with his new subjects. The people asked for some relief from the heavy burden Solomon had placed on them. Rehoboam started off well by consulting the elders his father had previously consulted. They said to him, "If you are willing to be a servant to these people today and give them a favorable answer, they will always be your loyal subjects." (I Kings 12:7 NLT). What great advice!

Unfortunately for Rehoboam and the people, he rejected that advice and instead sought the input of his inexperienced friends. These inexperienced friends were being influenced by their self importance and were beginning to enjoy the power they would have with their buddy Rehoboam as king. They believed the lie that their relationship with Rehoboam would produce many benefits for them if they advised him to use power. There was no focus on meeting the needs of the people, only on their personal pleasure and comfort. These inexperienced friends advised Rehoboam to be a power leader, not a servant leader – advice that was completely contrary to advice the wiser, more experienced elders provided. The outcome of this key mistake was not just more work for the people, but the division of the kingdom. Rehoboam was focused on serving himself and not others. He was a power leader, not a servant leader. The results were disastrous.

Yet another example is found in the lives of King Ahab and his wife Jezebel. In I Kings 21 we read that Ahab wanted to have the vineyard owned by Naboth. Naboth said no to Ahab and a pouting Ahab told his wife who had her own interests in mind. She wrote a letter in Ahab's name, using his seal to make it official. Jezebel had it delivered to the nobles who lived in the same area as Naboth making false accusations and demanding that they stone Naboth. The nobles followed what they thought were orders from King Ahab and killed Naboth. Since Naboth was dead, Ahab could then take over the vineyard *he* so desperately wanted. Once again, here is an example of a leader who was focused on himself rather than genuinely caring about others under his authority.

When leaders focus on themselves, there is a tendency for them to behave in ways that oppose God as well as oppose their human brethren. When this happens, there can hardly be a focus or concern for the eternal and Kingdom impact. God does not honor this behavior.

In all of these examples, there was selfishness, lying, murder and manipulation. There was a use of power, not authority or influence, to obtain one's own way. They used these techniques to accomplish something that would benefit only themselves and not others. With the focus on themselves, their perspective was purely selfish and temporal. Do these examples of people displaying selfishness, lying, murder and manipulation remind you of any so-called leaders of the modern day? It should, because there are numerous examples. As Christian leaders, we are called to behave and lead in a much different manner.

Lessons Learned about Servant Leadership

1. A servant leader does not control others, they provide for their needs so the greater mission can be accomplished.
2. A servant leader is not selfish or self-focused, they are humble *and* confident in their purpose and mission.
3. A servant leader takes a genuine interest in others under their authority.
4. A servant leader understands that the source of their authority is from God and not from their position title.
5. A servant leader is teachable and always learning.
6. A servant leader acts with integrity.

Practical Application

How can we be servant leaders in today's culture and environment? Let us explore some key qualities of servant leaders.

Servant leadership is serving your employees so they can serve the customer. All leaders realize that without customers, there is no business. Servant leaders ensure that all employees have the strategies, goals and objectives, clear communications, tools, equipment, resources and policies in place so the customer can be served well.

Servant leaders provide an environment and culture that allows employees to be the best they can be. Servant leadership is not about focusing on profits first; rather it is about identifying the needs of others and being of service to others to meet those needs. A by-product of serving others might just be profits. Serving your employees also includes providing adequate compensation for their services.

Servant leadership is establishing an organizational culture of openness. Servant leaders are sincere when they ask how they can be of service to their employee, customer, owner or the supplier. When they ask for feedback or suggestions, they do so with the sole intent of meeting their needs (not wants), making things better for the people they are serving and not themselves. Servant leaders are open to hearing what the employees, customers, suppliers and others are thinking and feeling about the organization. Servant leaders truly want to know how the organization can be improved so that the customer has a better experience.

Leadership is a spiritual gift. If you have been given the gift of leadership, it means that God has placed you in the role of a leader to have an impact on the organization that employs your services. You do not have to be "in the ministry" to exercise your leadership gift; rather, your ministry is where you are now – in your business, your company, your organization – wherever God has placed you.

After all is said and done, why are we on this earth? It is not to be successful in business or as a world-renowned senior pastor of a megachurch. The reason we are here is to glorify God and to live a life that enables us to have eternal life with Jesus, our Lord and Savior. We are here to encourage and influence as many people as possible to embrace that truth. That is what servant leadership is about. It is about modeling our behavior (acting with integrity) so others will follow in our footsteps and know the Lord Jesus as their Savior also. Anything else and we are focused on the here and now and not the eternal. Focusing on serving others is taking the focus off you and placing it rightfully on others, including God, to serve God's purposes and His glory.

At the beginning of this chapter, a "power" leader vs. a "servant" leader was introduced. Any time a leader is in a position of influence over another person, he or she is in a leadership position. This can happen as a parent, boss, colleague, pastor, teacher and so many other roles. This is an important responsibility, and God says He will hold us accountable for how we performed in this role. How will you perform? Will you perform as a power leader or a servant leader? Will you seek to be served or to serve?

A telltale sign of how you will behave is to carefully examine your motives. Are you motivated by being served, thinking that you deserve to be served, that you are better (smarter, more capable, more talented or gifted) than others? Are you motivated by what you can gain from the situation? Or are you motivated by the *sincere* desire to be of service to others; to help others develop; experience enjoyment as you see others succeed – knowing that your heavenly Father will provide for you as He always has done and as He promises to continue?

My friend Kent Humphreys has said, Jesus knows more about our business than we do. We see this in Luke 5. This is early on in the relationship between Jesus and Peter, and it is the first time Jesus asks Peter to go out again and cast his nets. Peter was out all night and had no fish to show for it. He tried to convince Jesus to rethink His suggestion. As a lifelong fisherman, of course Peter thought he knew the situation better than Jesus. You know the story – Peter did what Jesus asked him to do, and his nets were so overflowing with fish, he needed the help of his partners to bring the catch into the boat

Regardless of the organization you are with, whether it is a non-profit, for profit, public, private, family owned, start up, government, or education – and whatever your role – Jesus knows more about it than you do. He is sovereign in all things, not just some things. His method of servant leadership deserves some study and modeling.

Do we suddenly acquire and practice the servant leadership style overnight because we desire to behave differently? Probably not, as Peter demonstrated for us. As leaders, we have behaved a particular way all of our lives. We have learned our current leadership methods by observing, modeling and implementing the successful habits of others. Habits, whether effective or destructive, are hard to break. However, with a willing motivation, a desire to change, prayer and God's blessing, this can be done. It is a process of transformation.

Leaders Using Power Or Influence

As servant leaders we are called foremost to serve others. We can lead others in two ways. One method is to force our will on those under our authority through the exercise of 'positional power'. Arguably, this is not really leading others at all – it is exercising control. The other way to lead is with influence. Effective and lasting leadership is not about giving orders, controlling or using the power that comes with the position. Of course, successful leaders will sometimes issue orders because of an extremely urgent or emergency situation.

Leaders who use the power that comes with the position generally have a command and control, dictatorial or directive style of leadership. This style is best used in situations where there is an urgent need to have a lot of people follow very specific orders to carry out a plan or objective. Think of a military operation. There is an overall mission to accomplish, intelligence is gathered regarding the enemy's position, strength and capabilities and a specific plan is developed by the generals to be carried out by the officers and troops under his command. There is a time and a place for this style of leadership.

Recall the story in Matthew 8 when Jesus encounters a Roman officer whose servant was ill. The Roman officer described the command and control style of leadership. Yet he knew that in this situation Jesus could heal the servant without having to enter the house. When he mentioned this to Jesus, verse ten says that Jesus "was amazed." Why? Because of the Roman officer's faith that someone with divine authority as Jesus had could accomplish anything, including healing an ill servant, regardless of the circumstances or location. Jesus said He had not seen faith like this in all of Israel. Faith in someone as a leader does not come from the command and control style. It comes from a leader who sincerely cares about those who are under his or her authority.

Leaders can implement plans by means of demanding or threatening (power) tactics for those under their authority to take action. "Do what I say and do it now, or else ..." What is implied here is that the leader has the power to fire you or impose other negative consequences if you do not obey his commands. I know of a business owner named Dave who actually has a plaque on his desk that says, "It's Dave's way or no way." This is the exact opposite of servant leadership.

Leaders who lead by power can expect to receive exactly what they have asked for in terms of task accomplishment. They do not leave room for others to have an opinion, for they believe the leader is the one who knows best. Performance and results can be fairly predictable. However, performance will rarely, if ever, exceed expectations, and new ideas are seldom generated. Interestingly, leaders who lead by power generally focus on themselves and give themselves the credit for achieving the accomplishments. After all, it was their idea, their direction and their "leadership" that achieved the result.

The command and power style generally requires a leader to constantly follow up and micro manage the details to ensure the exact outcome is achieved. They do this because they do not trust their staff to deliver or perform to their exact specifications. Many times they lack the self confidence that would allow them to trust others on their staff. They really believe that no one can do it better. As the number of people under this leader's command expands, they must hire other subordinate leaders who will help with the micro managing.

Alternatively, leaders can influence others by using relational authority. This occurs when leaders take the time to blend the needs of the organization with the needs of their staff and build trusting relationships based on true concern for the people in their sphere of influence. As a result, the employees usually act above and beyond what is asked for by the leader simply because they know the leader cares about them. Effective servant leadership influences others by meeting their needs, building relationships and caring about them.

Leaders who lead by influence lead because they have earned the trust and respect of the followers by their previous actions. They do not use power. These leaders inherently know that to have others willingly give their buy-in to a plan or goal is much more successful than forcing or demanding commitment. And in the end, this approach requires less energy and is generally more effective, especially when the leader realizes and appreciates that other people under his authority might have better ideas.

Successful leaders influence others to achieve the targeted end results. They do not prescribe specific steps to take in order to reach the goal. They use their understanding of other people, including keen insight to identify specific ways to motivate each staff member and convince them by using well-developed skills of influence.

This influence skill should not be confused with manipulation. To influence others, one must have a vision and outcome in mind. They must also take into account the audience and how best to motivate, connect and relate to that audience so they will take ownership of that same vision. Manipulation, on the other hand, is about focusing on the outcome for the benefit of self only. The manipulative leader devises tactics that are generally not fully honest or ethical and sometimes provide false motivation to entice their followers to take a particular course of action. This false motivation might be in the form of fear. It might also come in the form of a promised or implied reward the leader has no intention of actually fulfilling.

Think of the great leaders of both the Bible and the modern day world. Are they known because of their significant technical talent in engineering, operations, finance, marketing or other functional disciplines? Or are they known because they are relationship builders? As one moves higher up on the leadership ladder, the skill at building trusting relationships becomes much more important than the continued development of a functional skill such as science, engineering, or finance.

An analogy has been made by several writers over the past few years, including Jim Collins and Ken Blanchard. Adapting what they have said to this examination of power and servant leaders, when success happens, power leaders look in the mirror and congratulate themselves, while servant leaders look out of their office and acknowledge the team for the accomplishment. When failure happens, power leaders look out of their office to see who to blame, whereas the servant looks in the mirror to take responsibility for the failure.

As Christians, when we build relationships based on trust, and we genuinely care about the other person, we glorify God. This also earns us the right (and privilege) to introduce Jesus to those people who we have worked with and built solid relationships. Without the solid relationships, we cannot hope to share Jesus based on our words only. The words alone will be perceived as hypocritical if our previous actions do not support them. When we behave as hypocrites, we do more damage when we try to share the gospel with others.

Leaders As Others Focused

Successful leaders are those who have a strong following behind them. They gain a strong following because they have the best interests of their constituents in mind. In other words, they have identified their constituents' needs. They are servants to their constituents. In this context, constituents are employees, management, customers and suppliers. These leaders generally are ones who do not take credit for the successes; rather, they freely and willingly give credit to the people who accomplished the goals.

One of the ways they focus on others is by building relationships based on caring and trust. They open themselves up to care about the other people they are leading. The researchers James Kouzes and Barry Posner share in their book, *Encouraging the Heart*, one characteristic that was common to all top CEOs they studied – affection. They found that in order to be an effective leader, one had to sincerely care for those they lead. One cannot care about another person effectively if they do not have a relationship built on trust with that person.

Jesus modeled that behavior for us like no one else could have possibly done. He is the CEO of His Church. This organization has been around for close to 2,000 years and is constantly growing in members. How many people claim to be followers of Christ? How many people claim to be followers of anyone else? The numbers are astoundingly different. Jesus Christ, along with His early and current followers, have developed a leadership approach, style and method that are second to none. Servant leadership is a large part of that successful approach.

In reality, today's successful leaders (as measured by the continued growth of their organizations, the achievement of the goals they set, the satisfaction of any stakeholder and other related measures) are servant leaders. Leaders might take different approaches, but the successful ones realize that they must serve their constituents and not simply give them a whole list of orders to carry out.

Servant leaders are neither selfish nor focused on themselves. They do not put their own interests before others (Philippians 2:4). Think of any of the leaders who have fallen from their leadership position in business, church or politics during the past decade or two. Was there much evidence of them focusing on anyone but their own power and reward? There might have been outward signs of "ministering" to others, yet a deep look into their motivations would prove otherwise.

Can you imagine where these organizations would have been if those self-focused leaders would have placed the interests of others (stockholders, employees, customers, suppliers) before their own? It is truly sad that so many organizational leaders do not follow this principle.

In his book, *Good to Great,* Jim Collins discusses the leaders who have led the companies that are classified as Great companies. He classifies a particular type of leadership style that he names "Level 5 leadership."

One of the key traits of a Level 5 leader, according to Collins, is that they "set up their successors for even greater success in the next generation whereas egocentric Level 4 leaders often set up their successors for failure." Leaders who are other focused are those who set their successors up for greater success. Leaders who are others focused are those who accept their responsibility for developing others to take their place; to do otherwise or to ignore this is a failure on their part. Leaders who are truly others focused fully embrace this reality.

Leaders As Teachers

The leader who serves others is also a teacher. The servant leader must provide an example of 'service to others' for others to follow. The servant leader must also provide a motivation for others to follow. That is where the "influence" behavior comes in to leadership. We have all heard the expression that some leaders have staff who would do anything for him or her. The military expression is that the troops will go blindly up a hill to follow a leader they respect.

In business and other organizations, the expression speaks about going through walls for someone they respect. These leaders have provided motivation to do something the staff might not necessarily fully understand. It is because they have such respect for the leader. They trust that the action the leader has asked is needed to accomplish some greater good. The staff is saying they do not necessarily need to know what that end result is, but they will press on to accomplish the task anyway. This trust is never because of "positional power." This trust is earned by the relationship building behaviors of the servant leader who keeps watch over the people he or she is leading.

Those who are familiar with teaching techniques understand that not all people learn by the same method. Some learn by reading, others by observing and still others by doing. In his book, *Teaching to Change Lives*, Howard Hendricks says that psychologists believe we can potentially remember up to 10 percent of what we read, up to 50 percent of what we see and up to 90 percent of what we do. A component of servant leadership is showing people by doing or teaching something yourself.

Setting the example is another way to demonstrate servant leadership. Actions do really speak louder than words. A message on a local church building says, "Your walk talks louder than your talk talks." This statement is so true! If we say something, yet do something else or neglect to follow through as we have promised, what do most people believe – our words or our actions? The servant leader fully understands this concept and puts it into practice all the time. They have earned the right to be called leaders not because someone has appointed or elected them but because they have gained people's trust and respect by their previous actions. Servant leaders take this to heart and actively teach others to do the same.

Leaders Are Calm And Patient

Servant leaders have their emotions and their ego in check. They are not leaders who have the goal of enhancing their own ego. They are leaders who provide service to others with the result being an enhanced life for all. Those lives are enhanced because someone fully understands and meets their needs.

This does not mean successful leaders are without emotion or passion. Certainly there are leaders who have achieved remarkable accomplishments partly because they could not keep their emotions in check. They might be able to impact their organizations for a limited time but cannot sustain that impact over the long haul.

Calmness and patience are characteristics of servant leaders whereas agitation and impatience are characteristics of self-serving and power leaders. Although we never observed Jesus in action when He was on earth, in reading the gospel accounts, we see that He was usually calm and patient. We never read of Him rushing His disciples to arrive at the next place on the appointment calendar. In one of the only times He displayed anger, Jesus cleared the temple of the money changers. He did not even display anger toward Judas for his betrayal.

Leaders As Long-Term Thinkers

Servant leaders stick to their mission by making tough decisions that do not compromise the long-term objectives in order to achieve short-term gains. They sometimes make decisions that actually sacrifice short-term gains for the sake of the long-term objectives. Unfortunately, many publicly-held companies are led based on the anticipation of how the Wall Street financial analysts will react to short-term financial results or other such indicators. Therefore, publically-held companies that need to raise capital make decisions based in large part on the impression these short-term results will make on Wall Street analysts.

Furthermore, many compensation packages are based in part on short-term stock price performance, even if the organization is losing money or market share. Jesus said in Matthew 6:19-21, "Do not store up for yourselves treasures on earth, where moth and rust destroy, and where thieves break in and steal. But store up for yourselves treasures in heaven, where moth and rust do not destroy, and where thieves do not break in and steal. For where your treasure is, there your heart will be also."

Servant Leadership

Self Assessment

Below are thirty statements that are indicative of servant leader characteristics and behaviors. As you read these statements, be aware of the first response that comes to mind and circle the number in the appropriate column.

Never – 1	Seldom – 2	Sometimes – 3	Usually – 4	Always – 5

1. I sincerely desire to serve the people who work with me.

        1   2   3   4   5

2. I value relationships more than tasks or accomplishments.

        1   2   3   4   5

3. I regularly seek feedback on my behavior and performance from those around me.

        1   2   3   4   5

4. When people give me constructive feedback, I try to not get angry or defensive.

        1   2   3   4   5

5. When people give me constructive feedback, I work hard to fully understand what they are saying.

        1   2   3   4   5

6. When people give me positive feedback, I try to accept it humbly and without pride.

        1   2   3   4   5

7. When people acknowledge any successes of this organization, I vocally give praise to God for the accomplishment, and then my team.

        1   2   3   4   5

8. I regularly speak about the core values of this organization to employees, vendors and customers.

   1   2   3   4   5

9. I strive to empower people to behave in ways that exemplify the core values.

   1   2   3   4   5

10. I am easily accessible to anyone in my organization who wants to meet with me.

   1   2   3   4   5

11. I allow others to hold me accountable.

   1   2   3   4   5

12. I look for the gifts and talents that people have when considering a role for them in this organization.

   1   2   3   4   5

13. I make time to mentor at least one person at any given time.

   1   2   3   4   5

14. Each of my senior leaders or key contributors has a mentor or coach available to them other than me.

   1   2   3   4   5

15. I willingly invest in tools and training for my team's growth, even at the expense of profits.

   1   2   3   4   5

16. I realize that my example speaks louder than my words.

   1   2   3   4   5

17. I willingly and honestly acknowledge my mistakes, misjudgments or poor decisions to others in the organization.

   1   2   3   4   5

18. I rarely express any anger I might have at an employee, customer or vendor in an inappropriate manner.

       1   2   3   4   5

19. Establishing and maintaining healthy relationships with others in this organization is critically important to me.

       1   2   3   4   5

20. I regularly offer to pray for and with employees.

       1   2   3   4   5

21. Most of my decisions are made with the long-term interests of employees and others I serve rather than short-term financial gain.

       1   2   3   4   5

22. I regularly equip and encourage others to give their best.

       1   2   3   4   5

23. I really know the strengths and weaknesses of each member of my team.

       1   2   3   4   5

24. Each team member has a personal development plan that I monitor with them regularly.

       1   2   3   4   5

25. I regularly put my team's needs before my own desires.

       1   2   3   4   5

26. When I see obstacles preventing my team from moving, I do something actionable to remove the obstacles.

       1   2   3   4   5

27. I provide an environment where my team can ask questions, share ideas and take risks as a way of learning.

       1   2   3   4   5

28. I regularly show and express my appreciation for the commitment made and effort given by my team.

1   2   3   4   5

29. I have developed at least one successor for every key role on my team, including my job.

1   2   3   4   5

30. I sincerely desire to serve rather than control.

1   2   3   4   5

Total your score here: _____

If you scored between 130 and 150 – Congratulations, you are well on your way to being a servant leader.

If you scored between 100 and 129 – You have made some great progress, yet have a way to go before truly becoming a servant leader.

If you scored under 100 – You are encouraged to examine your leadership motives and behaviors and eliminate those that are not contributing to a servant leader mindset.

Servant Leadership

Practical Steps to Exhibit Servant Leadership

As you read through and consider adopting some of these practices, take the opportunity to identify what you will eliminate from your current practice – if you need help in identifying what to eliminate, ask a trusted colleague, friend or advisor.

1. Each month, ask your direct staff to tell you something they want you to keep doing, stop doing and start doing.
2. Each week, take a few minutes to encourage each direct staff member.
3. Each week, take a few minutes to learn what is on the mind of five indirect staff members.
4. Start a prayer request list that is passed to employees weekly.
5. Consider offering Corporate Chaplain or related service.
6. Coach your employee through the problem solving of a particular issue – do not just tell them how to solve it.
7. Visit with a staff member in their office or workspace, not yours.
8. Take the staff out to lunch occasionally.
9. Stay late with others when a major deadline is upon them, not to supervise them, but to encourage them – go out and get a pizza for them; make a pot of coffee.
10. Work with each direct report on the development of one skill per year.
11. Take time to communicate one core value each week or month both by speaking the value and demonstrating it.
12. When food is brought in for a working lunch, take the waste basket around to each person when they are finished and collect their trash.
13. Make time to mentor someone at a lower level in the organization.
14. Fund an internal library of books, tapes and DVDs on a variety of topics such as leadership, Bible study, gardening, woodworking and other topics of interest to the employees, not just you.

15. Listen intently when someone speaks to you. Be single mindedly focused on what that person is saying, regardless of all the other burdens you are carrying at the moment.
16. Return all phone calls and emails within a prescribed period of time.
17. Ensure your outgoing voicemail message communicates an attitude of a servant leader.
18. Treat vendors as you do customers.
19. Always determine, discuss and accept what role you had when something went wrong. Realize that you could always have communicated more clearly or provided more resources or support.
20. Readily admits mistakes, misjudgments, poor decisions, etc. in front of others.
21. Tell everyone good morning when you come in and good night when you leave – not just your key people.
22. In any given situation, ensure your intentions are for the other person's long-term best interests even at the expense of your short-term profit or your benefit.
23. Create a benevolence fund that employees manage for the hardship times of fellow employees. Employees can contribute to it, and the organization can match it.
24. Commit to a half day community project each quarter or twice a year where all employees can actively participate. For ideas on such projects, ask a local church.
25. When scheduling appointments with your staff, seek to schedule the meeting around their schedule, not only yours.
26. Work hard to learn something new about each member of your staff each week, including their outside interests, hobbies, career goals, spiritual perspectives, etc.
27. Behave as though you always have more to do to serve your staff or the organization – it never ends; you never reach the finish line.
28. Regularly communicate the future vision of your department or organization in a way that relays your passion and engages and connects people.

29. With each decision you make, consider how it will impact your customers (both internal and external) as well as your staff. Will it serve them, or create more work for them? Will it make their life easier or more rewarding, or will it make your life easier?
30. Respect and honor other people's time by being on time for your meetings with them – all of them. Establish a culture where meetings end on time.
31. Take opportunities with those you interact with to show and say how you value and appreciate them.
32. Encourage each staff member to have a personal development plan and make a point to review their progress with them quarterly or semi-annually. Ask how you can help them achieve their plan.
33. Work on your continuous learning. Ensure your team is committed to continuous learning.

CHAPTER FOUR

COMMUNICATION

God gave us two ears and one mouth for a reason

Scripture Passages

- Simply let your 'Yes' be 'Yes,' and your 'No,' 'No'; anything beyond this comes from the evil one. (Matthew 5:37)
- My dear bothers, take note of this: Everyone should be quick to listen, slow to speak, and slow to become angry. (James 1:19)
- And you shall teach them the statutes and the laws, and show them the way in which they must walk and the work they must do. (Exodus 18:20)

Introduction

Why do we read one book, but let another sit on the nightstand for days? Why do we start counting the recessed lights in the conference room when one leader speaks, but really engage when another speaks on the same subject? Why do people walk out of your office after a long meeting and do exactly the opposite of what you just talked about? *Communication.* Effective leaders know how, when and why to communicate. They understand that all the performance, action and results that those under their authority obtain must begin with communication.

Most effective leaders spend considerable time thinking carefully and critically about the purpose of their message and how best to communicate that message to their audience, be it an audience of one or 1,000. They deliberately craft their message in terms their audience will understand, even if it means communicating in a style different than their own. They think carefully about the timing of their communication.

God was perfectly clear in His communication. During creation, He communicated what He wanted, and it happened exactly as He said. In communicating to the first man and woman, He spoke clearly (eat anything you want except from the one tree that I have clearly identified) and provided the outcome of disobedience (if you do, you will surely die). Clear communication prevents misunderstanding.

Jesus embodies good communication. He knew His identity (God's beloved Son), His message (the truth) and His audience (all of us). He speaks clearly, concisely and understandably to everyone, and His words have been changing lives ever since. Consider the phenomenal growth and longevity of His organization, the Church!

Communication

Biblical Foundation

In Matthew 5:37, Jesus delivers one of many instructions for effective communication for leaders – "Let your yes be yes and your no, no." In other words, be committed to what you are saying; do what you say you are going to do. The Pharisees said one thing and did another, and Jesus was quick to point out that they were hypocrites. Jesus knew His every move was being watched by the religious crowd. They wanted to catch Him not practicing what He was preaching so they could then spread negative commentary and damage His reputation. He knew His actions needed to match His words. We must also follow this approach.

He is also saying to be clear and concise in our communication. He instructs us to not add to our message any unnecessary words which will lead to confusion or misunderstanding; His messages were simple. Throughout the Gospels, He uses unforgettable illustrations to drive home His points.

Remember the wise man who built his house upon the rock? How about the wolf in sheep's clothing? Jesus demonstrated that He knows His audience and how they will interpret His words. He used illustrations that made sense to them in their day and in their typical surroundings to make sure His message was fully and completely understood. These people knew what would happen when new wine was placed in old wineskins, or when new cloth was sewn on old cloth to repair a tear. He knew the most effective way to communicate with them so they would understand what He was trying to communicate.

Jesus says that when we add unnecessary words, those words come from the evil one. When we add unwarranted flattery, when we exaggerate, when we make excuses or blame others without looking at ourselves, these are ways our words are not exhibiting love toward others. This kind of behavior is exactly what the evil one wants us to do. When others see this behavior in us, especially as Christian leaders, we are not demonstrating the fruit of the Spirit (see Galatians 5:22-23).

Even worse, our behavior raises doubts in the minds of others about the truth and reality of Christianity. The evil one delights in this conflict and dichotomy.

Jesus minced no words with those who were out to harm His reputation. One Sabbath day, Jesus and His disciples did not take time for the ceremonial washing before digging in for a meal. When criticized by the hard-hearted Pharisees, Jesus asked them why they broke God's commands for the sake of their traditions. He then called them hypocrites!

Jesus recognized that communication is a two-way street, so He often urges His listeners to *hear* Him. Remember his repeated call, "He who has ears to hear, let him hear" (see, Matthew 11:15, Revelation 2:7). He clearly told us to listen, to be attentive and not focused on or distracted by other things.

James teaches us to use our ears and mouth in the proportion that God gave them to us. He gave us two ears and one mouth, so we should listen twice as much as we should speak. He admonishes us to not speak when we are angry. Translated to the leadership role, James tells us to listen more than we speak and not to become angry when people make mistakes or do not carry out our direction exactly in the way we expected. Good leaders examine their own performance first when one on their staff makes a mistake. They look to see what role they had in the other person's failure to perform up to expectations. They first ask what they themselves could have done differently. Good leaders assess how effectively they communicated their expectations and will take responsibility for their failure to clearly communicate.

In Exodus, Jethro, Moses' father-in-law, provides Moses with what is required for an effective leader to communicate. Jethro said a leader must tell them the roles they have and the techniques by which they are to perform them. Included here is a requirement to clearly articulate and define the character, values and behaviors that are expected by those who want to be part of the organization.

Communication

Proverbs on Communication

If you are a serious student of Proverbs, you will know that the book provides a wealth of advice and teaching on many subjects including all facets of communication. Let's look at some of the sage advice all from the NLT:

The heart of the godly thinks carefully before speaking; the mouth of the wicked overflows with evil words. (15:28) *There is more hope for a fool than for someone who speaks without thinking.* (29:30) The common suggestion of these two proverbs is to think before speaking. This requires some forethought and some planning. The warning is clear – if we speak before thinking it out, there is potential for evil to come out of our mouths. We know there is really no hope at all for a fool, yet this proverb says that a fool is in better shape than the person who speaks without thinking first. This is said to establish a stark contrast and emphasize the point that it is so important to think before speaking. Thinking before responding is difficult, yet the Bible encourages and compels us to exhibit this characteristic.

A truly wise person uses few words; a person with understanding is even-tempered. (17:27) We all know people who we just love to listen to because, even though they might not speak often or say a lot, when they do speak, wisdom flows out of their mouth. They give a short message, a quick story, a brief analogy, and it is always packed with wisdom. Even more, they usually say it in such a simple manner, you are prone to say, "Of course, why didn't I ever think of THAT." These people also are generally even-tempered, and do not speak with a lot of flare or excitement. They are calm and confident, yet unassuming. In this verse, Solomon is saying that the wise and understanding person can be distinguished from others by two characteristics or traits: a person who uses few words and a person who is even-tempered. How do you measure up to these characteristics? If you are having trouble coming up with an honest assessment, ask some people who are close to you, and ask them to be completely honest with you.

Everyone enjoys a fitting reply; it is wonderful to say the right thing at the right time. (15:23) Everyone enjoys someone with a quick wit, yet sometimes that quick wit is a word or phrase that does not build a person up, rather it tears them down. Saying the right thing at the right time is important to maintain someone else's self esteem, to encourage them or to build them up. When you think about it, it is the act of a coward or a person who lacks self confidence who will offer the quick-witted response that mocks or berates another person.

If you listen to constructive criticism, you will be at home among the wise. (15:31) *To one who listens, valid criticism is like a gold earring or other gold jewelry.* (25:12) *In the end, people appreciate honest criticism far more than flattery.* (28:23) These three proverbs have a common element of being able to seek and accept constructive criticism. Simply stated, people should welcome constructive criticism as a way to continue learning and growing; while insecure people will resist such valuable nuggets. Insecure people might become defensive or offer any number of excuses rather than just listening to constructive criticism. For those providing the constructive criticism, it is always better received when the focus is on the facts and not on someone's personality. When done this way, honest feedback is very valuable. It is so valuable that its worth is equal to gold, which back in those days was the most precious materialistic element known.

Kind words are like honey – sweet to the soul and healthy for the body. (16:24) Kind words are used to build someone up, to encourage them and to recognize their good efforts, intentions or work. Most people like to receive kind words and have kind words said about them. Some might become embarrassed if too much is made of it, so one has to know how the person will take the words. Anything that is sweet to the soul and healthy for the body is a good thing and should be used often. Notice this proverb presupposes that the kind words are true words – not flattery, gossip, exaggerations or other false statements.

Communication

Spouting off before listening to the facts is both shameful and foolish. (18:13) The key message here is to fully listen for all the facts before responding to someone. When we are in listening mode, we are the recipient of the communication. When we "spout off" it can be a sign that we are not listening to the speaker. Spouting off might begin with a phrase such as, "Yeah, but..." Spouting off is usually a sign that you think your side of the story is more important than the other person's side. You are so intent on telling your side that you are not showing genuine care or concern for the other person. This leads to behavior Solomon calls "both shameful and foolish." When we respond before all the facts are spoken, we look like fools and our behavior is not endearing to the other person. As receivers of information we are instructed to fully listen to what is being said and to listen for understanding.

A gentle answer deflects anger, but harsh words make tempers flare. (15:12) This is particularly helpful in a conflict situation. If someone comes to you yelling or screaming at you for something they think you did or did not do, the natural response is to scream back at them. Proverbs advises otherwise – a gentle answer deflects anger. Remaining calm in any tense or conflict situation will help a great deal in deflecting anger and allowing both parties to address the root of the conflict.

The tongue can bring life or death; those who love to talk will reap the consequences. (18:21) *Watch your tongue and keep your mouth shut and you will stay out of trouble.* (21:33) Be mindful of what you say, how much you say (as opposed to how much you listen), and realize that there are consequences for what you say. If you want to stay out of trouble, limit what you say. What does this mean for a leader? An effective leader is one who communicates a message of vision, direction and values. He or she is seeking to have others follow by sending a clear and concise message that enables and empowers others to take a desired action. We become bored with leaders or speakers who drone on and on; we prefer the crisp messages that leave no room for doubt or misunderstanding.

87

Telling lies about others is as harmful as hitting them with an ax, wounding them with a sword or shooting them with a sharp arrow. (25:18) We know it is against the ninth commandment to lie. This proverb tells us the impact of our behavior when we lie, especially about someone else. The impact of an ax, a sword or a sharp arrow is a very visual description of what lying about others can do. As leaders, telling lies about our staff, our peers or even our boss can have a devastating impact on their trust of us. When we lose the trust of those we interact with, we can no longer be effective leaders, regardless of how good or talented we are. Lying about our competitors is also very harmful. We will eventually be found out and trust with a client or customer will be tarnished. We must also be careful to not omit critical information in our communication in order to obtain favor from our audience, or to inappropriately influence them in a particular direction. This is manipulation and is another form of lying.

Fire goes out without wood and quarrels disappear when gossip stops. (26:20) This is such a great comparison. When there is nothing to burn, the fire stops. When there is nothing for gossip to feed on, the fights with others will go away. While healthy conflict is good, conflict which is rooted in false information, gossip, and assumptions is unhealthy. Gossip is not just something we attribute to a meddling neighbor. We all know that if we desire to have a rumor in the office, we know who to speak to in order to start it. We are warned to stay away from gossiping in all situations.

Lessons Learned about Communication

1. Effective communicators plan out what they want to communicate before actually sending or speaking their message.
2. Effective communicators speak or write messages that can be clearly interpreted and understood by their audience.

3. Effective communicators speak to their audience in terms they (the audience) will understand.
4. Effective communicators use relevant illustrations and analogies to capture people's attention and to illustrate an important point.
5. Recipients of a message have a responsibility to fully listen to what is being said, void of any preconceived notions or distractions.

Practical Application

Communication tops the list of topics most frequently written about in relationships, management and leadership. We just seem to have real problems communicating. A world-renowned management expert, Peter Drucker, has said that sixty percent of all management problems result from faulty communication. As leaders, we must take ownership of our role to communicate clearly if we want certain outcomes achieved or results realized. It starts with the leader and our effectiveness at communicating our thoughts, intentions, and direction.

When I work with organizations on strategy and leadership issues, inevitably a client will say, "You know, Bill, we really have a problem with communication at this organization." Through the years of working with companies, organizations and people on these communication issues, I have come to the conclusion that the root cause of virtually any communication problem can be found in one of three areas – the message, the sender or the recipient.

In any communication event, we find ourselves as either the author of the message, the sender of the message or the recipient of the message. Many times we are at both ends of the communication line (sender and recipient) at different parts of the same conversation. How can we honor God and enjoy success in each of these aspects of communication? We will explore each of the three areas of communication next.

The Message

The message element of communication is simply the idea or point the sender wants to deliver to a recipient. For a message to be understood by the recipient, it must be clear, concise and exact in its meaning. There are many ways we can convey an idea or point. Generally speaking, the more complex the message, the more opportunity for our audience to misunderstand the idea or point we are attempting to communicate. Years ago, the popular terminology for communicating was to use the KIS method – Keep It Simple.

The simpler the message, the more likely it will be fully and properly understood. The message has to be tailored to the audience. The audience very likely has a different background as compared to the message's author. The audience may interpret words differently than the author intends.

Sometimes the author of the message wants to impress his audience by using words that show a measure of their intelligence. Many times, this backfires because the audience does not understand the meaning of such sophisticated words. In an effort to avoid the embarrassment of revealing their "smaller" vocabulary, the member of the audience does not ask for the meaning of the word and therefore misunderstands the message. A good rule of thumb is to use language that is appropriate for the person in the audience with the least developed language skills.

Use simple terms as you formulate the message, and you can rest assured everyone in your audience will understand the exact meaning of your message. Can you imagine the local radio weather forecaster saying, "We can expect the present atmospheric conditions to indicate a resplendent sky with a clement thermal reading to remain throughout the day" when he could have said, "Today will be a sunny day with temperatures in the 80s."?

Many companies have invested millions of dollars in developing their brand, a very compact message they want their customer to think of when given the opportunity. They realize their intended audience is bombarded with thousands of messages daily, and the brand helps the consumer remember the one key message about the product.

Ensuring the message itself is clear and will be appropriately understood by your audience is of paramount importance. If you fail to craft the message right, you might as well not send it at all. Of course no one does this on purpose, yet we often fail to think this important step completely through. To paraphrase an old adage, if we fail to plan our message, we should plan for our message to fail. Contrary to popular belief, and realizing how many of our communication events are spontaneous, we actually have more opportunities to plan our message before we speak. Just taking ten seconds to think wisely about how we can express the message in simple terms can mean a world of difference to the recipient, and can increase the potential for the person to fully comprehend what we are saying.

In our leadership roles, we are communicating messages all the time. We have to ensure our messages are clear because we do not have time to micromanage what people are doing to implement the directions contained in our messages. It takes time to craft a simple and clear message. That time is well worth the investment to ensure the message is crystal clear and will be interpreted exactly as it is intended. It is an amazing thing to know that we always have time to correct our mistakes, but we rarely have time to do it right the first time.

The Sender

The sender has a message to deliver to another person or group of people. He or she has a thought, idea, decision, action or some other message that needs to be transmitted to someone else. He or she can send that message in oral or written format. Speaking, writing or combining both of these in a presentation is the means by which the sender transmits or sends the message. We need to be perfectly clear and concise in the message we want to deliver.

If we assume our audience will figure it out, we are headed for trouble. We should not be surprised to see a person doing the opposite of what we thought we communicated. Our communication may also be misunderstood if we assume our audience is just like us.

There are several items to keep in mind as the sender of a message.

Defining Your Purpose

The sender must deliver a clear, concise and precise message that can be understood by the intended audience, whether that audience is one person or a 1,000 people. To do this successfully, the sender has to understand what the purpose or intention of the message really is and the most effective manner in which the audience will be able to understand it. This means that a sender's first task is to define the message's purpose.

Typical purposes include:
- Convey a thought or idea
- Request information
- Request a task or action be taken by someone else
- Initiate a discussion in order to obtain other ideas
- Ask for a decision or action
- Inform the audience of needed information
- Inform the audience of a decision

Deciding upon the purpose of your message helps you take the first step in composing and sending clear messages. It also helps the recipient understand your message. What happens when you convey a message to someone who does not understand your intent? If the sender does not clearly convey that the purpose of the message is to ask for a decision, the sender will certainly feel frustrated when they do not receive a decision. What about the sender who calls a meeting to generate ideas and meets with a silent audience because they believe they expected to receive information? The sender did not inform his audience of the purpose, so the audience did not adequately prepare for the meeting which led to an additional meeting and wasted time.

Communication

I recall coaching a Vice President of Business Development at a client company. One of the items we were working on was John's tendency to be verbose in both his verbal and written communication. In one of our meetings, John told me he had sent the CEO several emails regarding a particular project, but those emails were unanswered. I knew the CEO (Bob) of his company well and decided to ask him his side of the story. Bob responded that he hardly ever read any of John's emails because he did not know if John was asking for a decision, providing information or asking a question. Once I indicated that I was working with John on this area, we developed an approach that worked for both Bob and John and would allow John to prepare less verbose emails.

Make your purpose clear by stating it up front before each communication event. An agenda is a great tool for stating the purpose of your communication. The agenda does not need to be a formal document every time you communicate; however, you should state your purpose for each meeting to achieve good communication. You might have heard the advice given to those preparing a speech: Tell them what you will talk about, say what you want to say, then summarize what you have said to them. It is an excellent advice. You can start most informal conversations with a phrase such as, "what I would like to talk about is…" Share your purpose. For example, if your purpose is to communicate a decision that has been made, you might have an opening statement like, "I want to inform you of a decision that I have made regarding …" This gives the recipient an idea of what to expect to hear and this helps them tune out other potentially distracting thoughts.

Communication Styles
    You may be familiar with a four-box model that describes four personality styles. They use terms such as

- Driver- Expressive-Amiable-Analytical (Merrill-Reid)
- Dominance-Influencing-Steadiness-Compliance (DiSC)
- Choleric-Sanguine-Phlegmatic-Melancholy (Hippocrates)
- Lion-Otter-Golden Retriever-Beaver (Drs. Gary Smalley and John Trent)

    There are similarities to communication style as well. For purposes of this discussion, let's use the Driver-Expressive-Amiable-Analytical model. Here are some personality and communication characteristics of each style:

Driver	Expressive	Amiable	Analytical
• Get things accomplished • Cut to the chase • Direct and pointed • Likes to be in charge • Action oriented • Makes quick decisions • Will take risks • Can be abrupt • Usually in a hurry • Self-starting • Like to delegate • Doesn't take time to teach • Opinionated • Extroverted	• Love to talk • Abstract thinkers • Creative • Like to influence • People centered • Poor listeners • Lots of energy • Extroverted • Optimistic • Fun-loving • Gregarious • Quick thinkers • Lots of gestures • Sense of humor	• Nice people • Responsible • Reserved • Logical • Cooperative • Persistent • Good listeners • Like to be of service to others • Relaxed and easy going • Steady temperament • Like to take time in making decisions • Dislike confrontation	• Quantitative • Perfectionists • Must have the facts • Critical thinkers • Like the details • Resist change • Low risk takers • Follows the rules • Introverted • Task oriented • Few gestures • High standards

    After looking at these characteristics, you may find that you have characteristics across all four styles, but your predominant style should be reflected in one or two of these styles. Many results-oriented leaders fall into the Driver style. Some sales- or marketing-oriented leaders fall into the

Communication

Expressive style. Many service-oriented leaders exhibit Amiable style characteristics. Many technically-oriented leaders fall into the Analytical style.

Part of the value of looking at four different styles is to realize that people are different. This means that their personality and their preferred manner of communication is different. One style is not necessarily better than another; it is simply how God has designed us from the beginning.

The following chart will provide some tips on communicating with someone who has a style different from your own.

Communicating with a Driver	Communicating with an Expressive	Communicating with an Amiable	Communicating with an Analytical
• Say just what they need to hear • Stick to the facts • Resist the small talk • Stick to business and the matter(s) at hand • Be well prepared • Have an organized package • Start with high level and go into details only if needed • Don't take it personally if they interrupt or want to move you along	• Provide a warm, friendly environment • Ask about things that interest them • Put details in writing so they can review later if needed • Allow time for them to go off on tangents • Ask "feeling" questions • Be fast moving, stimulating and creative	• Begin with a personal comment to break the ice • Present your case softly and in a non-threatening manner • Allow them time to think about how the information will impact their relationships • Present ideas and goals logically • Don't rush them into making a decision, especially if it involves confrontation with another person	• Prepare your case in advance • Stick to business • Keep emotions to a minimum • Show facts and statistics to support your findings or position • Be accurate and realistic • Be straight-forward • Have action plans in writing • Allow them time to ponder the information before reaching a decision

While these Communication Styles are not an exact science, they can be quite helpful in providing you with some tips on gaining better results from your communication experiences. They will help you prepare more understandable messages as you begin to appreciate the others' differences.

Knowing Your Audience

Once you have defined the purpose of your message, you must decide how to communicate it with the greatest impact. This depends largely on who makes up your audience. Use the communication styles guide to help you craft your message.

Understanding your audience is critical to effective, clear and accurate communication of the message. Think about some communication problems you have experienced in the past. Now consider how well you knew your audience. Did you have a good idea of how the audience would receive your message? What was their background? What was their perspective on the subject? What preconceived notions might they have about the subject? What was their level of comprehension, and were you using language that was appropriate to their level?

We often communicate a message the way we would like it communicated to us. This approach will not work if the audience is not like you. You would speak differently to a 5-year-old child than you would to the head of a major corporation. They are different people, with different levels of comprehension, different perspectives and varied backgrounds. The 5-year-old lacks the mental capacity of the executive. If you approach each person you communicate with as if they had the same knowledge of the subject as you do, you are promoting misunderstanding and confusion. Knowing this, you should tailor your message to ensure that your audience has the best possible chance to grasp it. If your audience does not understand your message, why communicate it in the first place? If your audience does not understand your message, you are to blame, not them.

Suppose you have a Driver communication style. You would like to discuss some thoughts you have been having about future direction of a product or division. If you want to deliver this message to someone who is an Analytical style, you must descend from fifty thousand feet and provide some facts, figures and statistics in keeping with your purpose. If you do not adjust your approach, your Analytical audience will think your message is too broad and not well thought out. They will likely dismiss it as irrelevant or unimportant.

Conversely, if you are the Analytical person sending a detailed, well-thought-out message to a Driver, you probably will lose that person within the first few minutes of your conversation. They are lost in the initial details.

Since our language is so complex and ripe with opportunity for misunderstanding, successful communicators regularly use examples to help clarify their point. They typically use everyday examples their audience will recognize. Many communicators use sports analogies. This is helpful in some cases; however, it might not clarify your point when an audience is not familiar with that particular sport.

The Method of Delivery

Selecting the method of delivery is also extremely important. Verbal forms of communication are most effective when you want to deliver a message and obtain some sort of reaction. The reaction can come in the form of a discussion, agreement or commitment to a future course of action. Verbal delivery can occur face-to-face, by telephone, by video or presentation to a group. Verbal forms of communication allow the sender to gauge the reaction of his audience, and use voice pitch, tones, and emotions such as excitement or enthusiasm to assist in the meaning of the message.

Written forms of communication are best used when you want to convey a message that is definitive (i.e., you do not want any discussion because the decision is made or the policy is now official) or you are asking for some response from your audience. In the latter case, you are allowing the audience to ponder the message(s) for a time and expect to receive their comments, either in verbal or written form. Written forms of communication are useful when you want your audience to think about some items before meeting together to discuss them. Written forms of communication are also useful when the subject must be documented, as in a policy or directive. The Old Testament Law is a great example of this.

Written forms of communication must be developed carefully to ensure your message is communicated exactly as you intend. Reviewing your written message before sending it guards against someone misunderstanding the message. Asking others to review the message before it is sent and seeking their feedback on how they interpret the message further reduces the opportunity for misinterpretation.

You can enhance understanding of verbal and written messages when you include illustrations. Jesus, the world's most effective communicator, often used illustrations to clarify His messages. We have all sorts of analogies we can use to help illustrate our point. Of course, the analogy must be understood by the audience. Jesus spoke to Peter, Andrew, James and John about fishing because they were fishermen. He used analogies of shepherds because people understood the job of a shepherd.

We have many options in illustrating our messages today, with the availability of graphics, cartoons and other visuals. A picture *is* worth a thousand words and can be a wonderful way to illustrate a point; just make sure your audience will interpret your illustration the way you intend. Personally, I tend to comprehend a lot more when hearing a message presented by my Pastor when he can utilize various graphics, video and other technology to enhance the message he is sending. Have you ever attended a church service in another location, heard a message that was delivered in a unique manner, much different than you were used to hearing? If you have had that experience, chances are you remember more of that message, regardless of whether you agreed with the content or not. Effective communicators know how to use a variety of delivery modes to enhance the understanding of their messages.

Many people now prefer to initiate or continue a conversation using email or text messaging. In many cases, however, these technologies have significant drawbacks. Any written form of communication, including email, can create misunderstanding. The sender and the audience lose the visual and emotional element so useful in verbal communication. Keep this in mind when you, as the sender, compose and deliver your message. Emails can help you provide information without an expectation for a response or ask a simple question. More complex messages are best delivered verbally whenever possible.

Email is arguably one of the better technological advances of the recent past; however, it has created new patterns of communication, not all of them efficient, effective or healthy. For example, leaders in some organizations receive one hundred or more emails a day. They need several hours a day to read and respond to them. Executives need assistants to read through, sort out and prioritize the many messages they receive. And this tool was supposed to make our lives more productive! Instead, we have added several hours to our day. Why? Because in some organizations email has become the tool of choice in communicating with our colleagues even if they have the office next to us. We want others to know what is going on so the quantity of people who are copied on email messages continues to grow. Many times, people who are copied on a message feel compelled to respond. This initiates a new round of emails to all the people on the original message. In addition, the new message has been sent to others who should be in the know. And another vicious and highly unproductive cycle is created.

I had a call from a client not too long ago asking for my opinion on how to respond to an email she received from a colleague. My client needed the assistance of her colleague to finish working on a project that she was assigned. She sent her colleague an email requesting certain information. The colleague responded in an email by asking my client to perform some particular tasks that she felt were really her colleague's responsibility to perform. My client was preparing her response and wanted to run it by me to make sure the message she was sending was clear, but not overbearing. My advice? Visit your colleague and discuss this in person. After all, he sits in the office next to you!

We often fail to realize that email can take longer to communicate a message than the verbal form. Email definitely has a place in communicating; we just need to manage this tool so it works for our benefit. A simple rule of thumb is if an email is sent back and forth three times and either the sender or receiver still needs clarification, stop using the email method and make an attempt to speak to the person verbally via telephone or in person.

We have become accustomed to receiving messages with lots of color, excitement and use of different approaches to attract our attention. With apologies to Microsoft, we can imagine some companies that have come close to banning the use of PowerPoint to deliver messages. In these cases, the focus has clearly become the delivery of the message as opposed to the message content itself. I recall being told of a situation where a client wanted to have what they perceived as a simple meeting with a consultant who was helping out on a project. The client was quite frustrated when the consultant wanted some extra time to put together a "deck of slides" that he deemed necessary for this simple meeting. The client viewed it as overkill, yet the consultant was too distracted by the technology to focus on creating a clear and precise message.

Ensuring Your Audience Understands

The sender must ensure the audience has properly understood his or her message by asking for feedback, looking at the audience (even if it is only one person) for signs of understanding or confusion, and based on follow-up conversation gauging whether the audience fully comprehended the message. It is the sender's responsibility to ensure the message is accurately understood by the recipient.

Imagine the sender of a message in a room of ten colleagues. Can the sender accurately gauge if the audience understands her message if she is looking at the floor of the room rather than looking at the people who are receiving her message? Of course not. As a sender, we must actively seek signs from our audience that they fully comprehend the message we are attempting to send them.

We tend not to plan or give much thought to our email responses. As a result, our messages are misunderstood and result in more emails being sent back and forth. This is especially true when we treat email messages more informally than we do other forms of written communication, such as the more formal memo or letter. We tend to allow shortcuts and looser use of grammatical standards when composing email messages, particularly responses to emails from our colleagues.

However, we have all re-read an email we wrote and saw a typo or realized we could have worded our reply differently. Just as much care should be given when composing messages using email, because it is still your responsibility as the sender to ensure your audience has the best chance of clearly understanding the message you are sending. In addition, since you may not have full control of who else might read your message, it is incumbent on you to ensure clarity.

I have a pastor friend who was preparing to give a presentation to the Board of Elders at his church. The topic had been discussed for several months, and he wanted to move the topic along and have the Board make a particular decision. A lot of information had been given to the Board. In addition, as one of the champions of this particular proposal, he had been quite busy gathering supporting information from a wide variety of sources both within and outside the church.

When it came time to make the presentation, he thought it would be helpful to begin the presentation by ensuring everyone was on the same page as to where they were in the process. This was an important step to take up front because some of the Elders had been involved all along and others had not participated that much. His purpose was to provide enough information for the board to make a forward-moving decision. He had to make sure that all the attendees had the same information with which to make that decision. Can you imagine what would have happened if some of the Elders brought different perspectives into the meeting? We have all been to those kinds of meetings, whether in a church or corporate setting, and the result was terrible. Because he was careful in planning his message and ensuring all the attendees were on the same page, the action he sought was taken, and it was a successful communication event.

Many times, a message's sender makes the fatal flaw of assuming that everyone in their audience has the same information or same perspective regarding a situation or issue. They then begin to ask for a decision or some other action, but fail to realize that some people in the room do not have the same perspective of the facts. In short, not everyone is ready to buy into the concept as they lack information that others might have.

This creates more work for the sender of the message because s/he has to communicate many more messages just to avoid the confusion. If the entire audience is not on the same page, the desired outcome is jeopardized; there will naturally be different thought patterns at work due to different information received by each person about the subject matter.

My pastor friend took just a few minutes at the beginning of the meeting to ensure everyone was on the same page i.e., he set out an agenda. Part of the agenda was to reach a decision by the end of the meeting. He took some time to ensure each one in his audience had the same information thereby increasing the chances they would have the same perspective. When it came time to ask for the decision, everyone was prepared and equipped to make one.

The Recipient

A recipient's job is to hear and understand the intended message. This is difficult to accomplish if the recipient is not listening, is focused on how he or she is going to respond or is judging the message sender. As recipients of a message we frequently feel we must put our interpretation or spin on the message. The Pharisees were experts at this technique of thinking how they were going to respond or hearing what they wanted to hear and not what Jesus was actually saying.

Effective recipients develop the key skill of active listening, which is the ability to focus on what the sender is intending to communicate, hearing the words and the nonverbal cues the sender is transmitting. Paraphrasing is part of active listening. Effective recipients are consciously aware of their preferred communication style (Driver, Expressive, Amiable, Analytical) and make an appropriate adjustment to their style when they are on the listening end of a conversation.

Jesus demonstrated active listening many times as He would repeat or paraphrase what someone said and then provide His own response. He also knew His audience and how they would use His message. Many times in the Gospels, we read about a situation and how Jesus knew their thoughts or knew their intentions. Obviously, He had a divine ability to read thoughts and intentions of others that we do not possess. Nevertheless, He has taught us to be attentive to the meaning that others are trying to convey to us.

One of the ways we can better understand the sender is to try to read them. You can learn and hone this skill. Most of us have an ability to sense when others are listening to us or are uninterested in what we are saying. We can assess their level of understanding of our message by the questions they ask or the body language they exhibit.

We know someone is listening to us when they provide affirmative responses such as, "I understand," "I see," "yes," 'tell me more" or when they provide nods of their head or facial expressions that indicate understanding. Contrast that with the deer caught in the headlights look, or the blank stare that people often display when their mind is not focused on the sender.

The recipient's role is to listen for understanding. To listen does not necessarily mean you have to agree with what is being said; rather, you are listening to hear what the sender has to say. The recipient is not listening if they are thinking about their response or thinking about how they do not agree with what is being said. The recipient is also not listening if they are forming their objection to the message without fully allowing the sender to deliver the full content of the message. When recipients are distracted by random and unrelated thoughts, they cannot be fully attentive to the message that is being sent.

Have you ever had to back track as a recipient when you have formulated an opinion based only on partial information from the sender? You have to state your opinion, only to be embarrassed by the sender when they inform you that you either did not allow them to finish or did not hear their entire message.

As leaders, we have a tendency to want to be in control. The more in control you want to be, the less likely you are to listen intently.

As a leader, if you have a driver style, your behavior as a recipient is likely to be looking for the key issues and the facts. You would prefer to have this delivered to you in as quick a time as possible, because you are action oriented and you have a lot going on. As such, you are likely to seem impatient when the sender is not a driver. This is generally not the way to model Christ-like behavior in your leadership role.

Ineffective leaders do not listen to what is being said by their staff because the leader has the incorrect notion that they (the leader) should be knowledgeable about all matters. These leaders usually drive their companies to ruin. The best leaders exhibit humility by indicating they do not know all the answers and are genuinely interested in what others have to say.

Effective Bible study takes into account the context of the passage before developing an interpretation. We must do the same as a recipient of messages that others are sending to us. As recipients we must look at the message whether it is sent in verbal or written form from the perspective of the sender.

Communication Ethics

All of this discussion assumes you want someone to understand the messages you are sending and you yourself desire to understand others. Unfortunately, we can be tempted otherwise. Not all communication is created equally. Good communication is an ethical issue. Words, grammar and punctuation all work toward one goal – saying something worth saying and providing your audience a fair chance at understanding its intended meaning.

The problem is that we sometimes do not want the truth or the reality to be fully understood so we employ vague verbs and nonsense nouns. Corporate leaders will take the lead of their public relations staff and put a positive spin on seemingly negative information so the feared Wall Street analysts do not change their minds and recommend the company stock be put on the "sell" list. Profits are off, yet the spin will be that "management is aggressively looking at the cost structure of the business" to ensure profit targets are met in the future.

We find other examples in our politicians all the time. A reporter will ask for their position on a particular issue and the sugar coated words start to fly. Even the average listener knows the politician is trying to wiggle out of taking a firm position on the issue. Political-speak, or being politically correct, has no place in the behavior of a Christian leader.

Jesus said to give it to them straight. Let your yes be yes and your no be no. We are commanded not to be deceitful in our communication. We know the Lord hates a lying tongue. Proverbs 12:22 (NLT) says, "The Lord detests lying lips, but he delights in those who tell the truth." This goes for all of our communication with others. When information is passed on to others that is intentionally incomplete or paints an inaccurate picture, we are guilty of deceit. If we take the attitude that we can not control how people will interpret the message, we are really on questionable ground as far as ethical communication is concerned. The truth sometimes does hurt. However, we will be held accountable for every word we utter, even for the false words, the misleading words and the incomplete truth.

Communication includes ensuring your nonverbal forms of communication (such as behavior and body language) agree with and support the words you are speaking. The impact of your words can be nullified by what you convey nonverbally. Your actions will contradict your words and cause your message to be misunderstood as in the case when you tell a struggling employee that you are committed to her success while offering no encouragement or plan for helping her meet your expectations. Your nonverbal message communicates louder and clearer than your verbal message. Make sure the two align so your mixed messages will not collide.

As Christian leaders, we seem to be under a microscope. We proclaim to be followers of Christ, and we are enthusiastic about the future. The non-Christians around us want a way to disprove us, so as the Pharisees did, they watch for opportunities to damage our reputation by pointing out that we do not practice what we preach. There is not one of us who is perfect, yet we must press on and establish behaviors that minimize the opportunities for our detractors to call us hypocrites. We need our yes to mean yes and our no, no. We need to commit to do what we say we are going to do. If you say you will return a call, return the call. If your outgoing voicemail message says you will return calls and you do not necessarily return everyone's call, especially sales people, you might want to consider changing your outgoing message.

Communication can be one of the toughest challenges you face as a leader. Skilled communicators are not easy to find today; however, all you need to do is to focus on the three basic principles of the message to communicate effectively.

Practical Steps to Exhibit Effective Communication

Here are some practical steps for you to consider. As you read through and consider adopting some of these practices, take the opportunity to identify what you will eliminate from your current practice – if you need help in identifying what to eliminate, ask a trusted colleague, friend or advisor.

1. Determine your preferred communication style and the style of those you interact with most frequently. Identify ways to modify your style to match the style preferences of others.
2. Develop a chart indicating the communication style of those in your organization who you deal with frequently, such as your boss, your staff members, your peers and others. Next to each name, identify one or two traits about them, and in another column, indicate how you will approach them differently because of their preferred style.
3. Respect every individual you communicate with regardless of their position.
4. Intentionally speak to individuals on their terms and resist forcing it to be on your terms.
5. Whenever possible, plan before you speak.
6. Praise in public, correct in private.
7. When providing performance feedback, focus on the facts and not on the person's personality.
8. Ensure your communication is fact based – not assumption based.
9. Always know the purpose for your message.
10. Resist or eliminate the habit of multi-tasking when you should be listening to what someone is trying to communicate to you. Do not respond to email messages when on the phone with someone or while in a meeting.
11. Evaluate your performance after communicating a message. Did you achieve your purpose? How were you assured that the audience fully understood your message?
12. Evaluate your performance as a message recipient. Did you provide your full and complete attention to the sender? Did you exhibit active listening techniques?

13. Actively coach and encourage your staff to enhance their communication skills.
14. Ask for feedback on written messages before you send them. Obtain feedback on the clarity of the message and whether the intended audience will understand the intended meaning.
15. Ask your staff for feedback and suggestions as to how you can better communicate with them. Do this monthly.
16. Never respond to an email or phone call in anger or when you are upset. Cool off and answer when you are more clear-headed.
17. When a string of email messages reaches three responses, and the issue remains unresolved, commit to visit or call the person to bring the matter to a conclusion.
18. Make it a habit to personally evaluate or assess the communication skills of others; learn from what they do well.
19. Practice communicating in a style that is different from your preferred style.
20. Ask a trusted colleague or staff member to give you regular feedback they observe when you are either the sender or recipient.

===

CHAPTER FIVE

===

LEADERSHIP DEVELOPMENT

Building the leadership pipeline

Scripture Passages

- "[C]omission Joshua and encourage and strengthen him, for he will lead the people across the Jordan. He will give them all the land you now see before you as their possession." (Deuteronomy 3:28 NLT)
- "David said, 'My son Solomon is still young and inexperienced. And since the Temple to be built for the Lord must be a magnificent structure, famous and glorious throughout the world, I will begin making preparations for it now.' So David collected vast amounts of building materials before his death. Then David sent for his son Solomon and instructed him to build a Temple for the Lord, the God of Israel." (I Chronicles 22:5-6 NLT)
- "Again He said, 'Peace be with you. As the Father has sent Me, so I am sending you.' Then He breathed on them and said, 'Receive the Holy Spirit.'" (John 20:21-22 NLT)
- "You have heard me teach things that have been confirmed by many reliable witnesses. Now teach these truths to other trustworthy people who will be able to pass them on to others." (II Timothy 2:2 NLT)

Introduction

Why have some organizations been able to grow and prosper for decades or even centuries? Of course there are many reasons for this, but one of the most compelling is the intentional and ongoing commitment of leadership development – the ongoing commitment to build and train leaders to take the place of the current leaders and carry on the mission and purpose of the organization. Centuries ago, God knew this to be true; the Bible is filled with examples of leaders training, mentoring and developing other leaders to take their place and allow God's vision and purposes to continue.

Leaders do not just appear. They cannot all of a sudden be appointed and expected to succeed without adequate training and preparation. Just because someone is six foot ten inches tall does not automatically make them a NBA basketball professional. They need other skills to be well developed before they can reach this level of performance. Just because someone can throw a football fifty yards does not automatically make them a star quarterback for a football team. Other skills, such as communication, decisiveness, and leadership need to be well developed before this person can be successful as a quarterback.

The son or daughter of a family-run business is not automatically qualified to be the founder's successor to the founder merely because of their genealogy. Significant leadership skills must be developed if this person is to be successful as a successor. We will see that this process of training and mentoring takes a great deal of time – years, not weeks or months. In our Leadership Development Survey, 90 percent of the almost 600 respondents indicated that leadership development was either essential or important to the organization's success. Yet, only 60 percent indicated that their organization's efforts regarding leadership development were either "very dedicated" or "dedicated." This is alarming when we think about our responsibility as leaders to train up the next generation of leaders.

Leadership Development

Developing effective leaders is arguably a chief executive's most important role and should receive the most attention. Sadly, this is not always the case. People are appointed to leadership positions who are not qualified or ready, and organizations that were once successful begin to flounder. Highly talented, motivated and loyal employees begin to leave. Core values and customer satisfaction begin to erode, and the very survival of a once thriving enterprise is at stake.

This scenario does not have to happen, but it takes significant focus and commitment, careful planning and a willingness to confront reality in order to avoid what has happened to thousands of organizations. How can we avoid a leadership vacuum in our organizations? God's model for building the leadership pipeline is a great place to begin learning.

Biblical Foundation

Have you ever noticed that God is the one who actually appoints leaders? Consider the appointment of the following biblical leaders and prophets – Abraham, Joseph, Moses, Joshua, David, Solomon, Elijah, Elisha, Jonah, Peter, John, Paul, and Timothy. All were appointed by God. He also allows the appointment of leaders who do evil. We know that God is sovereign in all things. His allowance of leaders who do evil is not because He was busy doing other things or was not paying attention. It is because He wants to accomplish something specific, and He will use a particular leader to do the very thing(s) He wants accomplished.

God let Moses know well in advance that Joshua was His selection to succeed Moses. God instructed Moses to invest time in training Joshua in a variety of skill-building areas. Some of those areas included being a military commander and learning how to select other leaders. As Moses' apprentice for many years, Joshua learned all the requirements God detailed for building the Ark of the Covenant, the Tabernacle and the Altar. He learned all the functions and requirements of the priests. On many occasions, Joshua had the opportunity to experience God firsthand with Moses as he took Joshua with him.

Moses taught Joshua by giving some of his authority to Joshua (see Numbers 27:20). Moses informed all the people that the next leader was going to be Joshua. He publically declared Joshua as his and God's choice – the leader who would finally take them into the Promised Land.

Above all, Joshua was equipped with a firm belief in God and a perspective that included God and what He had in mind. Go back to the report Joshua provided as a spy the first time the 12 spies went into Canaan (Numbers 13 and 14). Ten of the spies looked at the situation from their own perspective, and they let fear of the unknown come into their judgment and assessment. Although they acknowledged the land did indeed flow with milk and honey, they were overcome with fear by the sight of fortified cities and men who looked like giants. Joshua and Caleb saw it from a different perspective. They saw it from God's perspective. Numbers 14:8 (NKJV) quotes Joshua as saying "If the Lord delights in us, then He will bring us into this land and give it to us." He continued in his encouragement by saying the people should not fear man but should be aware the Lord was with them. Joshua had a God-perspective. God-appointed leaders have a God-perspective –especially when it comes to addressing seemingly impossible challenges.

In its footnote on the II Chronicles 6:24 verse, the *Encounters with God Daily Bible* general editor Dr. Thomas Blackaby notes, "God speaks to us through our circumstances. When God allows us to experience failure or continual defeat, He may be sending us a strong message. It is foolish to endure continual hardships and yet not seek the Lord for an explanation." This is applicable for leaders as well. If we as leaders are experiencing failure or continual defeat, (and what leader has never experienced failure or defeat?) what is it that God might be trying to say to us? What is it that He wants us to learn? Leaders who seek the Lord for an explanation for their failures and troubles have a God-perspective on their leadership role.

The leadership building process Moses provided to Joshua took years; communicating and influencing skills had to be developed. Moses did not just send Joshua to the Hebrew Management Association to take a two day workshop on influencing. Moses understood that this was far too important to delegate to someone else or to outsource to another organization. Moses took the time to invest in Joshua so he would be assured that Joshua learned what Moses knew he needed to learn.

Moses' final step as he transferred leadership responsibilities to Joshua was to take the public step of informing all the people and letting them know that Joshua was now in charge. He encouraged Joshua to "be strong and of good courage" and reminded the people that God had selected Joshua to lead them into the Promised Land (see Deuteronomy 31:7-8). Moses knew how to give up control in such a way not to confuse the people. Everyone knew that Joshua was in control now. No one went to Moses after that to try to override some command Joshua had issued.

This is an important principle for leaders who are developing other leaders. Although God clearly told Moses his time was up, Moses did not sulk about it. He did not create a "Chairman of the Hebrews Emeritus" position for himself. Moses did not set up an office to remain on the premises or otherwise make himself available for the people to seek his counsel. He knew God's plan for himself, for Joshua and for the people and graciously and humbly followed that plan. He knew if he continued to hang around the office, Joshua would not be able to effectively lead the people. Many current day leaders need to follow this wonderful example.

Deborah is another example of a leader who led, developed and encouraged an up-and-coming leader. Deborah, as we read in Judges 4, was a prophetess who was also judging Israel. In this leadership role, people from Israel would come to her for decisions on matters they could not decide among themselves. The Israelites would disobey God and God would deliver them into the hands of their enemies. Yet in His sovereignty and unconditional love, He would raise up judges to rescue them from those who were oppressing them. This was a cycle that was repeated many times.

Since Deborah was a judge, God had selected her to lead the people out of the oppression of Jabin, the king of Canaan. Judges 4:3 tells us that Jabin had ruthlessly oppressed Israel for twenty years. Deborah had a word from the Lord to call Barak and have Barak lead some of the Israelites into battle against Jabin's commander, a man named Sisera. Deborah called Barak, who must have had a leadership role among his tribe, and told him about the Lord's directions. She began to develop this leader and to prepare him to take on the larger role that God had ordained; he was to lead 10,000 men to battle against Sisera.

Barak must have lacked self-confidence and sought encouragement and reassurance from Deborah. He told Deborah he would not go into battle unless she accompanied him. Deborah must have heard another word from the Lord who foretold that Barak would not receive the glory for the victory. His lack of self confidence and lack of trust in the Lord's plan would enable a woman, later identified as Jael, to be in a position to actually kill Sisera and gain the glory.

Barak was a leader that God had ordained to lead a battle that would result in their deliverance from enemy rule. Barak seemed to lack the self-confidence to fully carry out this assignment without help from another leader. Deborah provided the necessary encouragement and reassurance to boost Barak's self confidence. Effective leaders do what is necessary to build other leaders by recognizing what the up-and-coming leader needs in order to be successful.

It is clear that God had appointed Solomon as the next king of Israel even though David acknowledged that Solomon was young and inexperienced. David did what was necessary to equip Solomon so he would be successful. David, in reality, did not really have too many other choices. His first son Ammon had a significant character flaw with morality for he was the son who raped his half sister, Tamar. The next in line was Absalom. Unfortunately, his character flaw allowed him to take matters into his own hands not once but several times. First, he responded to the rape by killing his half brother, Ammon, for what he had done. Next, he grew impatient for David to step aside as the king, and he initiated a rally of the people to challenge his father for the throne.

Here is a lesson for those who want to pass the leadership mantle onto their children. While that may be the expected thing to do, in addition to carefully assessing the skills and abilities of the children or other relative, the character of those individuals must receive serious scrutiny. It seems that every year, at least a few high profile executives, whether in public service or corporate service, have fallen from their positions because of a character flaw that probably did not develop while they were in their powerful position. Rather the character flaw that existed became excessive and uncontrollable because of their powerful position. The temptations were too great. As a result, they lied, cheated, stole, and had extra-marital affairs or a host of other offenses (sins).

David had many deficiencies during his reign as king. However, one thing he did well was to prepare Solomon for success. In addition to the materials and skilled workers he provided, David also prepared his key advisors to be available to guide young Solomon. David engaged the help of Zadok the priest, Nathan the prophet, and Benaiah the commander of David's guards among others to come alongside Solomon in his early days on the throne. David also advised Solomon to be cautious with those he would rely on for advice. This included Joab, the army commander, who killed in peace as well as in war.

The most important way David prepared Solomon for success was in providing his final instructions to his son, found in I Kings 2. David instructed Solomon to, "keep the charge of the Lord your God: to walk in His ways, to keep His statutes, His commandments, His judgments, and His testimonies ... that you may prosper in all that you do ..." (I Kings 2:3 NKJV). David knew that all the human skills or talent Solomon had would be worthless if he did not first walk in the ways of the Lord. David advised his young son to keep God's statutes and not have his own interpretation of the statutes, as still happens so easily today.

As I write these words, I am reminded of some phrases in a letter Chuck Swindoll, the gifted Bible teacher, has written in a recent letter to friends of his ministry, Insight for Living. He is commenting on the fact that the world is changing from standing firm on ethical and moral boundaries to becoming tolerant. He writes,

> There was a time – I remember it well – when prayer was a daily occurrence in every schoolroom, Presidents quoted from the Bible, pastors preached straight from God's Word, and people treated Scripture with reverence. But times have changed. *The ignorance of biblical knowledge in our society is rampant ...* Instead of interpreting life honestly, we are now encouraged to view it emotionally and to act accordingly. Our thinking is no longer based on the objective truth of the Bible.

This is what David was advising his son more than 3,000 years ago. He was admonishing and pleading with him to walk in God's ways, to keep His statutes, commandments and judgments. David was instructing his son to steer clear of what the world would have him do, believe and accept.

Solomon, as you know, turned out to be the wealthiest and wisest leader of the world, in large part because he did follow the statutes, commandments and judgments of God. It is unfortunate that he did not always follow those ways; he did succumb to the world's ways in worshipping other gods and doing things that were acceptable to man but detestable to God, which eventually led to the fall of the kingdom.

As we look at many examples of training and building up the next generation of leaders throughout the Old Testament, it is clear that the older generation can have a significant impact on the younger generation. We have seen that this impact can be very positive or very negative. While they do not have ultimate control, (only God does because He alone appoints leaders for His purposes) the older generation of leaders does have an incredible opportunity to influence them, and that includes positive as well as negative influence.

Jesus served as a model in building leaders. Jesus spent about three and a half years in His public ministry. And, boy, did He ever develop leaders who would go on to change the world! While He spent time educating the citizens of Israel about the Kingdom of God, He took the time and effort to teach, train, mentor and build up those who would take over for Him when His time on Earth ended. While He instructed thousands, He spent most of His time with twelve. Three in particular received His intimate and concentrated time and experienced His teaching, mentoring and experiential time. He set up an experiential learning program for seventy as He sent them out to preach. His entire method of building the leadership pipeline was very purposeful and specifically planned out.

As Christians, we know Jesus' main mission was to die on a cross to pay the price for mankind's sinfulness. This was the only acceptable solution to a Holy God who cannot tolerate disobedience. If you think about it, this could have happened in a day or week. Why then, did Jesus spend thirty three years on earth? He spent that time to model for us how to live. He spent the three-plus years in His public ministry training leaders to carry out the growth of His Church. He knew that as humans, we would need time to learn how to be a leader God's way.

God could have written a book and said this is the way I command you to be leaders, to be politicians, to be plumbers, to be doctors, etc. He has done that in some respects in the Bible, but He also created us in such a way that we learn more effectively by watching someone and by modeling some of these things ourselves so we can learn from them, especially the mistakes.

Jesus pointed out the flaws in the Pharisees' leadership model. He called the Pharisees a bunch of hypocrites as they had completely missed the key points of leadership that had already been written about; instead they focused on the images others had of them and making themselves look good in the eyes of others. Jesus told these Pharisees that their self focus and the importance they placed on their external image was no way to lead.

Jesus taught the twelve by spending quality time with them, going over the days' events and asking them what they thought and how they interpreted those events. When they got it right, He praised them; when they were mistaken, He gently corrected and set them straight. He gave them examples to follow; He edified their ability to understand the Scriptures because, next to direct contact with Him and the Father through prayer, He knew the Scriptures would be the best source of information for answers to many questions they would have after He was gone. By the way, that technique (prayer and seeking the Scriptures for counsel) is still very applicable and necessary to today's godly leaders.

When Jesus was teaching the seventy He sent out, (Luke 10) he provided specific direction as to what to do and what not to do. He warned them of the dangers they might face. When they returned, He encouraged them, praised them and told them how fortunate they were to see the things they saw. In other words, He had them evaluate their experience in a way that they learned, for surely they would face similar and even more difficult leadership challenges in the future. He knew this personalized experience would be an effective teacher in times to come.

Have you noticed that Jesus spent a great deal of His time training His future leaders as opposed to performing the work of the leader? He knew His role was to prepare others, not to be busy doing work or reading staff reports and checking off a long personal to-do list. This, too, is a strong lesson for us as leaders today. We must spend our time on those items that provide the best long-term impact – training up the next generation of leaders to adequately prepare the organization to grow and thrive according to God's plan.

Jesus also made sure that a successor or group of successors was identified, prepared and adequately trained to take His place. His final words to Peter were to clarify His expectations of Peter. In John 21, when Jesus asked Peter if he loved Him, He was asking if Peter was fully committed to Him and therefore the mission of the church – to make disciples of all the nations, baptize them and teach them to observe all of what Jesus commanded. When Jesus was assured that Peter was fully on board with the program, only then did He give Peter the assignment of being His successor. As Christians, we know that Jesus knew how Peter would respond – God had already appointed Peter when Jesus said that upon this rock, He would build His church. Jesus also knew that *Peter* needed to know without a doubt that he was committed to the plan.

Jesus equipped the leaders He trained. As the passage in John 20:21-22 points out, He breathed the Holy Spirit on His disciples, thereby equipping them and providing the tools necessary to be effective leaders. Without the Holy Spirit, they (as well as we) could not have been empowered to do the work they needed to do.

Jesus knew that not all of His twelve direct reports would work out and continue on in leadership roles. Judas was the one who had the character flaw that could not be overcome. Jesus knew about the character flaw, yet still chose Judas not for His sake, but for our sake – to teach us that we better have back up plans to our leadership development and succession plans. Despite our best efforts at assessing, training, mentoring and developing people, there will be some who, for a variety of reasons, will just not work out.

The Apostle Paul was a real mentor to Timothy. The fact that Paul could write a letter to Timothy (II Timothy) and provide some real teaching, encouragement and skill building can be a lesson to us today about being a mentor. Being an effective developer of leaders and mentor does not always have to be face to face – it can be by phone, letter or other more technologically popular techniques today. In Paul's day, email and Twitter were not available, so he used the power of the hand-written word, even if it was on parchment!

Timothy was a young and somewhat inexperienced leader (pastor) of a church in Ephesus. Paul knew from earlier encounters as well as from information he had heard from others that Timothy might be feeling somewhat timid in his leadership role. First, Paul encouraged him by reminding

Timothy of the faith that Paul observed and the solid foundation Timothy had thanks to his mother and grandmother. He reminded Timothy that God was the one who appointed him to be a leader and that God was the one who had given Timothy the leadership gifts required to do great things in Ephesus.

With Timothy, as well as others who Paul mentored, he demonstrated that in developing leaders, the focus must be on their strengths and not their weaknesses. He built up their confidence. He did not tear them down by focusing on mistakes or "developmental opportunities." In many of his letters, he would comment on the strengths of others who were leaders with him in his ministry. In the end of his letter to the Romans, Paul had a positive comment to say to many people he was sending his greeting to; he acknowledged at least one strength about each one.

Paul seemed to always be traveling with someone. He rarely, if ever, traveled alone. During that time, although it is not formally recorded, Paul no doubt spent much of that time pouring into those who were accompanying him. While he might have been discussing current events with them, he was certainly using that time to mentor, teach and train people in the Good News of the Gospel. While he was in prison, or traveling under guard, he regularly spoke to the guards about Jesus. He was always in a mentoring and teaching mode.

Paul encouraged Timothy to focus on several tasks as a leader. Paul told him to be aware of opposition and to make sure he kept the faith and did not compromise on the foundational truths. Timothy was instructed to, "Avoid worthless, foolish talk that only leads to more godless behavior. This kind of talk spreads like cancer … In this way, they (those who he gave as examples) have turned some people away from the faith" (II Timothy 2:16-18 NLT). Paul instructed Timothy to be careful about what he said and who he was listening to because some would misconstrue what was being said for their own purposes and wellbeing. This kind of foolish talk will be like a cancer.

As leaders, we must be very aware of what we say to others, especially those who look up to us. We must also be very aware of who we rely on and where we turn to obtain our advice. If we are not careful, we can be unduly influenced by the world view that sometimes speaks much louder than God's still small voice. Proverbs reminds us of this wisdom as well.

Importantly, Paul urged Timothy to teach others so they would be leaders as well. Paul knew that for the church to grow, leaders must be trained, mentored and multiplied. He charged Timothy with this responsibility – to not just focus on the growth of his own church in Ephesus, but to teach and train up other leaders in the right way so the greater church would grow, expand and enable the gospel message to spread among all the nations.

Lessons Learned about Leadership Development

1. God is the one who appoints leaders; He is the one who must be the author of any succession planning chart.
2. Development of leaders requires an investment of time and money; it is not an overnight process. In fact, it will take years to properly equip and develop leaders.
3. Successful leadership development is a multi-faceted approach of teaching, coaching, mentoring, encouraging, learning from mistakes and publicly empowering the up-and-coming leaders.
4. Back-up succession plans are a necessity, not a luxury as unplanned or unexpected events must be anticipated. Expect some preferred leaders to not be available because of a variety of circumstances including death, moral or character lapses and other life events.
5. Legacy leaders must learn to completely let go of the reins of power, authority and influence when their time has come; this is imperative if the next generation leader is to have any chance of success.
6. Leaders realize that one of their primary responsibilities is to train up other leaders to take their place to ensure the mission or purpose of the organization succeeds beyond them. They willingly subordinate their own pride and ego for the sake of the success of the organization.

7. Leaders who have failed to develop leaders under them have failed as leaders; they have also failed the organization that has entrusted them as leaders and failed God who appointed them in the first place.

Practical Application

The first realization we as Christians must have is that God appoints leaders. This is clear in the biblical accounts of how leaders came to be leaders. We must submit the selection of our organization's leaders to God in prayer and seek His counsel, plan and direction. Proverbs 13:10 (NLT) comes to mind: "Pride leads to conflict; those who take advice are wise." Another Proverb (16:9 NLT) provides good advice as well, "We can make our plans, but the Lord determines our steps."

When selecting leaders, we will make mistakes when we choose to make that decision without any input from other godly people or by utilizing various information sources to clarify and validate our thinking. It stands to reason that an objective assessment must happen prior to the selection or promotion. The assessment must include obtaining counsel and advice from other wise, godly people who share in the overall vision of the organization. This is a process that will take time and should not be rushed into for any reason.

Interestingly, 86 percent of the respondents to our Leadership Development Survey indicated they would be interested in an objective process to assess the capabilities of their leadership team. Chief executives or other leaders who believe they are sufficiently wise in their own knowledge and experience to select and develop leaders by themselves are sadly mistaken. These decisions are made by people with a great deal of pride who trust their own instincts. In reality, these people have their own agenda and rarely is this agenda aligned with God's agenda for the organization. Those mistakes inevitably cost hundreds of thousands if not millions of dollars. These kind of selection mistakes can be the forerunner of an organization's failure.

CEOs of family companies who automatically select one of their children as their successor, simply to keep the business in the family, often make fatal mistakes as well. Without utilizing careful selection criteria, without submitting the selection to prayer and seeking God's plan, these selfish or self-centered decisions lead to disaster and quite often the demise of a once thriving organization.

Selecting leaders who are just like us is also a strategy fraught with errors. Aside from the obvious possibility of one's swelled pride and ego leading to "like me" bias, selecting people who are just like us limits what the organization can do and limits where God might want to take the organization. We must select leaders based on what has to be accomplished in the future, not what has been accomplished in the past.

When selecting and developing leaders in a Christian-run organization, it is critical that those leaders are like-minded in their faith and walk with Jesus. Scripture tells us to not be unevenly yoked (II Corinthians 6:14). Paul was speaking to the Corinthians in a variety of contexts, including in a business or organizational arrangement. Ensuring that a leader's heart is aligned with God's eternal objectives is an important and critical criterion for selection into a leadership role. Leaders who are not evenly yoked will tend to have different and oftentimes conflicting values about what is important.

Leaders who have different principles or moral values will inevitably take the organization to places that God does not intend for them to go. This is painfully clear in the Old Testament when recording all the kings who came after Solomon in both Israel and Judah. For an organization to achieve what God has intended, it must be populated with leaders who believe in and follow God's principles to the core. Doing it any other way, while it might lead to temporary success or accolades, will surely lead to longer term failure.

We are told in Scripture that God will hold us accountable for our actions. This is certainly applicable to us as leaders. In every leadership development or selection decision, why not have as one of your filters determining if Jesus will say, "Well done, my good and faithful servant."

Building a pipeline of leaders requires a committed plan and a process. As discussed in the Biblical Foundation section, leadership development takes an investment of time. The development of leadership skills must have a goal in mind. What specific leadership skills need to be developed? Before answering that question, one must ask what specific leadership skills are needed. The accurate identification of specific skills that are needed is the first step and can differ from organization to organization.

Leaders must commit to spend some of their precious time developing leaders beneath them. If you are the CEO, then your responsibility is expanded to ensure the organization as a whole spends the appropriate amount of time and resources on developing its leaders – both current and next generation leaders. The CEO is accountable for ensuring the overall leadership development strategy is well-defined and works effectively to achieve its targeted goals. If a leader is not spending time developing other leaders, he or she will have failed in his or her full leadership role. Leaders must develop other people to take their place; to not do so is a sign of self-centeredness, short-term thinking and pride that no one can replace you. That is not honoring God.

Common Leadership Development Tools and Practices

Leadership development is accomplished most effectively when a variety of approaches are utilized. Here are some of the most common and successful tools and practices for you to consider for you and your organization. Proverbs 29:19 reminds us, "A servant cannot be corrected by mere words; though he understands, he will not respond." In other words, sending an rising leader to a training program, even though it might have exceptionally strong content, cannot be relied on exclusively to build that leader's competencies.

Leadership Competencies

Moses recognized Joshua needed development in some key competencies and skills. Many organizations have identified the development of leadership competencies as a foundational tool in their leadership development strategy. This is a best practice where particular competencies are identified as being necessary for successful performance in a leadership role. Competencies are defined as abilities, behaviors and talents that can be consistently described, measured and assessed. In this context, abilities are learned skills such as strategic planning or finance; behaviors include elements such as time management, communication and interpersonal conduct; and talents are those elements that are natural for a person, such as detail orientation, creativity or energy.

Within each competency are proficiency levels that are identified as appropriate for successful performance. Actual behavior that is below the desired proficiency level will lead to less than successful performance; similarly, behavior that is an overuse of the competency can also lead to performance that is not successful.

For example, suppose a leadership competency of "providing direction to staff" is established. The desired proficiency level would include the establishment of clear and measurable goals, providing clear information as to the desired outcome of a project or task and defining clear measures of successful performance. If someone demonstrates this proficiency, they would be considered successful in this competency. Someone who demonstrates behavior that is below the proficiency may not have goals for their staff or might withhold necessary information needed for the effective performance of a task.

On the other hand, someone who is overusing this competency would demonstrate it by exhibiting very controlling and micromanaging behavior or by holding to the strictest standards so the staff is actually constricted from performing at their best. Recall Jethro's advice to Moses in Exodus 18 about delegating. Moses thought he was the only one who could settle the people's disputes. This was an overuse of a competency that became a weakness. Jethro predicted that unless Moses trained others to do this role, Moses would wear himself out.

Competencies can and do differ from organization to organization. Mirroring what works for one organization will not necessarily work for another organization because the purpose, mission, values and strategies might be different. It is important to establish competencies based on the needs of a unique organization.

Assessments

Leaders today would benefit from tools that help us make good decisions about a person's leadership competencies. Assessments are very useful tools to help objectively identify the current proficiency level and compare it to the expected or desired proficiency level of particular competencies. Assessments exist in many forms and as such, some are much better than others.

Assessments are only as good as their proven validity in assessing or measuring what they purport to assess or measure and their applicability to your leadership development objectives. For example, some of the more popular assessments such as Myers-Briggs and DiSC are best used for team building or understanding temperaments of individuals. They are not as effective when assessing competencies.

Assessments can be found in the form of personality and psychological assessments, skill and ability assessments, interest and preference assessments, and others. Assessments are best used to evaluate competencies when they can measure a leader's style, ability or interest against the specific competencies that the organization has defined as necessary for successful performance of its leaders.

Some assessments have been developed that do a very good job at assessing a number of leadership competencies. When considering an assessment to use, be cautious of the specific competencies and the definition of those competencies. If an assessment tool defines "providing direction to staff" differently than your organization defines this competency, the usefulness of that particular assessment will be far less. Do not be tempted to modify your definition in order to force fit the use of a particular assessment tool. Make the investment to continue your search for an assessment tool that will provide real and lasting value for your organization.

360 Feedback Surveys

Consider Proverbs 15:31-32 (NLT) "If you listen to constructive criticism, you will be at home among the wise. If you reject discipline, you only harm yourself; but if you listen to correction, you grow in understanding." We all need constructive criticism to learn how we are being perceived by others. This is not so we can adapt to other's expectations of us, rather for us to be on a continual path to model our leadership behavior to that which God expects.

360-degree feedback surveys are a viable tool to use to obtain constructive criticism, as well as positive feedback. With this tool, a survey is given to a leader and those who would form a 360-degree circle around that leader, i.e., his boss at the top of the circle, his staff at the bottom of the circle, and his peers, clients or others on either side of the circle. The *participant* of the survey is the individual leader, and the *raters* are the boss, all the direct staff members, and three to eight peers.

Typically, the input or answers to the survey questions provided by the staff and peers are kept confidential; their input is consolidated, averaged and presented to the leader in summary form. Additionally, there is generally a place for the participants to express candid comments anonymously and is designed to provide insight as to how the leader is actually perceived in a particular competency area. To many who utilize 360 surveys, these comments can be the most valuable data collected.

The survey design is important. The areas included in the survey should be tied directly to the competencies the organization has determined are necessary for successful performance by a leader. Each competency area should have from five to ten questions or statements that are intended to provide a complete picture of the leader's proficiency within that competency. Some surveys utilize the question format, while others utilize a statement format. Both are equally effective.

In the design of the statements or questions, it is important to ensure that only one question or statement is being asked or made. For example, if the competency area is *communication* consider a statement that reads, "Is clear and concise in all communication." The rater might experience the leader as clear in written communication, yet not so clear in verbal communication. Or they might experience conciseness in written but not verbal communication. This is an example of multiple statements being made in a single statement and will result in inaccurate responses by the raters. A clearer way to make this statement would be to break it into several statements such as, "Is clear in written communication," "Is clear in verbal communication," and "Is concise in verbal communication."

Generally, a scale is provided for the rater to use when answering the question or responding to the statement. As I have used in the Assessment section of several chapters in this book, the rating scale can be an indication of the presence of the particular skill or trait and is expressed on a range from "Never" to "Always". Another common scale is "Strongly Agree," "Agree," "Disagree" and "Strongly Disagree."

The data is then collected, summarized and provided to the leader in a way that provides trends and insights regarding how the leader is perceived by others in the various competency areas. The data is generally collected by someone who can keep the information confidential, or in many cases, a third party who can administer the entire process. A tailored development plan can be put together using some or all of the various tools discussed here. The 360 survey instrument, if designed and administered appropriately, is highly recommended as a way to benchmark leaders and can be updated on a yearly basis.

As with the assessment tools discussed above, there are some well-designed off-the-shelf 360 instruments. In determining whether to use an off-the-shelf instrument or design one for your organization, be sure to assess the coverage of those competencies that are unique to your organization in the off-the-shelf tool. They might be measuring competencies that are defined differently than your organization's competencies or are not as important to you. If this is the case, the value you receive will be far less.

Coaching and Mentoring

Sometimes, the best approach to develop leaders is to provide professional coaching or mentoring. These are two different approaches, although sometimes they are confused as being the same. Mentoring is generally done within an organization, where a senior, more experienced person is either asked or volunteers to be an informal advisor to an up-and-coming leader. The mentor provides the mentee with insight and counsel and acts as a sounding board to the mentee. When done well, this relationship fosters significant growth in the mentee and significant satisfaction for the mentor, because the mentor can give back some of what he or she has learned through many years. Think back to the discussion of Paul and Timothy; this is an outstanding example of mentoring.

The mentor will impart their knowledge of the organization culture, their insight as to the skills, temperament and style needed to succeed in the organization and be an objective interpreter of the impact of particular decisions affecting the mentee. The effective mentor-mentee process is typically based on the mentor asking questions of the mentee that require deep reflection and insight; this enables the mentee to take time to process key information about how they respond, act and behave in particular situations, thereby learning how to approach certain leadership challenges in the future.

Professional or executive coaching is sometimes conducted internally, but most often it is a service provided by an outside consultant who specializes in this field. Coaches are effective when they can assess a leader's strengths and weaknesses (or areas for development as some like to say) and develop a tailored plan that will help enable the leader to maximize their strengths and minimize the impact of the weaknesses. There has been a great deal of research on this topic of maximizing strengths and minimizing weaknesses. Suffice it to say that effective coaches can help enhance what

God had originally put into the person and not try to correct what God left out. After all, God put in or left out particular skills, traits and behaviors for His perfect reasons.

Coaches will conduct their own assessments of the individual generally using many of the tools mentioned here. They will provide candid and direct feedback to the coachee regarding their skills, traits and behaviors. For coaching to work most effectively, the coach must understand the competencies that the organization has determined are necessary for successful performance and work with the coachee and the coachee's manager along those lines. Additionally, the ability to build a trusting relationship is critical. The coaching environment is not to be confused with psychological counseling; however, there might be times when similarly sensitive and personal information is shared by the coachee.

All this discussion about mentors and coaches presupposes that the leader is committed to receiving advice and counsel from others, whether they are from inside or outside the organization. They must be motivated to receive this insight or the mentoring or coaching process will not be successful. They must also be committed to listening to others' points of view. Mandated coaching or mentoring is generally not successful for this reason.

Peer Advisory Groups

Today's leaders have organizations available to them that equip, encourage, mentor and develop leaders from different organizations as they meet together in a peer advisory group. Typically, these groups are comprised of eight to twelve leaders from various organizations who meet on a weekly or monthly basis. Some are for CEOs only and the topics discussed are centered on issues facing typical CEOs. Other groups have various levels of leaders. The members of these peer advisory groups commit to actively participate, encourage one another, pray for one another and hold each other accountable for demonstrating and practicing biblical principles in their personal and leadership lives. Following customized instructional material, the members learn about a myriad of business, leadership and organizational topics that are biblically based. The groups follow the principle of 'iron sharpens iron" and encourage its members to live an integrated Christian life 24/7.

For businesses, two organizations offering peer advisory groups are Fellowship of Companies for Christ International (www.fcci.org) and C12 Group (www.C12Group.com). Both organizations have excellently prepared content. You are strongly encouraged to join an organization like this as a part of your leadership development plan.

Experiential Learning

No doubt you are familiar with the expression "experience is the best teacher" as an effective way to develop particular skills. As with all leadership development, experiential learning must have a plan, purpose and desired outcome. As mentioned in the *Communication* chapter, many adults learn best by doing or performing something rather than reading or hearing about how to do something.

Many people learn best by the mistakes they make. This is a very effective method of development, as long as the mistakes are not significantly costly to the organization. You might be familiar with the story about an IBM executive who made a million dollar error. When Thomas Watson, the CEO was asked if the executive was going to be fired, he reportedly replied, "Are you kidding, I have just made a million dollar investment in this man and I want to get a return on that investment."

Some larger organizations use experiential learning as an intentional leadership development strategy. They might assign an up-and-coming leader to a position where he or she will be immersed in a particular environment or situation that will help them learn a particular set of skills or be exposed to particular cultures. Assigning the leader a role in an overseas location so they can learn the culture of that country is another common method for the leader to gain valuable, hands-on experience and perspective.

Smaller organizations apply experiential learning by assigning the leader to head a project team in order to learn skills of delegation, project management or collaboration. The work itself is important, and the leader receives the benefit of learning and enhancing a particular skill or two as well.

Experiential learning must be carefully planned with goals and measurable learning objectives. This must be monitored to determine if the objectives are being met according to the desired timetable. Adjustments might have to be made along the way as we can rarely anticipate all the events impacting experiential learning. As with coaching and mentoring, the specific experiences should be tied to the competencies the organization has determined are necessary for successful performance. Learning for the sake of learning is generally not an effective use of precious resources.

Succession Planning

Going back to the Leadership Development Survey, only 19 percent of respondents had a written succession plan in place. Of these, only half of those believed such a plan was appropriate for the business at the time the survey was conducted. There are many reasons for this, some of which you may identify within your own organization. Some of those reasons, which I refer to as *myths*, are discussed below and presented with some realities leaders should consider.

Myth *The organization is mine, and I do what I want with it.*

Reality As Psalm 24:1 says, "The earth is the Lord's and everything in it, the world and all who live in it." If you are a Christian, the organization is not yours. It belongs to God, and you are a steward. If God has given you an organization to run for Him, chances are good that He does not intend for it to end when you retire, become disabled or die. While that is always a possibility, God has a pattern of establishing things for generations, so that they can have an eternal impact. Do not neglect your role as a steward of what God has given you. This will be discussed thoroughly in the last chapter of this book.

Myth *My organization is too small to have a succession plan.*

Reality If you have five or more employees, even if they are all family members, the prudent decision is to have a plan. Most leaders have life insurance. They might even have disability insurance. Many probably have a will (which by the way is not a nice-to-have, it is a must-have). Having these tools in place is one indication the leader cares about the ones they love and want to provide for them in case something happens to them. Succession planning is about planning what happens to the organization and employees in case something unexpected happens to the leader that will either temporarily or permanently incapacitate the leader from performing ownership or leadership functions.

Not having a plan creates unnecessary risk to the livelihood of the employees and their families. Having addressed the financial aspects by having a large life insurance policy that will cover the bills and maybe provide some operating cash for awhile is one aspect of effective succession planning. What about the leadership needed to continue to run the organization? A CEO of a small business or family-run business places an undue burden on his or her spouse to run the organization in the event of an absence, when the spouse is neither interested in nor fully capable of assuming this responsibility.

Myth *I do not have time to write out a plan.*

Reality If this is the logic, then this leader probably places little value in budgets, marketing or sales plans, business plans or goals. The old saying, "if you fail to plan then you plan to fail" seems appropriate here. Succession planning is not just about the top job either. A worthwhile succession plan takes into account all key positions within the organization, not just the CEO position.

Most leaders do not plan for their key staff to leave, become disabled or completely incapacitated. Unfortunately, life happens and when we are not prepared to handle the consequences, we tend to be in a reactionary mode. A succession plan is proactive. When we are in the reactive mode, our options tend to be quite limited.

It is not that leaders do not have the time to develop a plan. The real reason is that they do not want to make some key, potentially hard and uncomfortable decisions.

Myth *I do not know how to create a plan.*

Reality   What is really being said here is that the obvious choices are not acceptable to the leader. It might be that the younger brother, child, or other second in command is not really ready to assume the top role. There might be disagreement among the family member partners on the talent of the nephew. Unfortunately, if there is not a viable alternative, or the partners are avoiding a "family conflict", nothing is done hoping that the business will continue to plod along and this succession thing will work itself out in a few years. These situations are not just limited to family-run organizations.

Partnerships and closely held organizations can face this situation as well. The ownership of a company generally gets together because each person has some unique talent they bring to the entity as a whole. As the entity grows, the realization sets in that greater talent or leadership is needed to sustain the organization. Failure to come to grips with this reality is like putting your head in the sand. Succession planning can be an objective process that can guide the owners and the key leaders of the organization to make the best long-term decisions to protect the viability of the company.

Myth *I do not think it is important.*

Reality Unfortunately, this is just an excuse for not making the serious decisions one has to make to give the future viability of the organization a fighting chance. Those who really do not think it is important to plan for the longer term are more likely focused on short-term results. This causes one to have a survivalist or reactionary mentality that does not think too far into the future and plan for the inevitable obstacles and roadblocks that businesses encounter. Those who do not think succession planning is important may be focused on themselves and what they can obtain and not the other employees or customers that rely on strong, forward-thinking leadership.

Myth *The issues raised in a succession planning process are complex and sometimes too difficult to discuss.*

Reality This is true, yet it is not a good reason to avoid tackling these problems. Financial considerations are significant, tax consequences are too. Most leaders would rather make their own decisions about their financial matters rather than allow the government to intervene. The issue of coming to grips that Junior is just not cut out to run the business, or that some family members would be offended by selecting a particular person, are difficult issues to address and resolve. They are uncomfortable at the least and loaded with potentially unhealthy conflict that can last for years. Not actively addressing these issues is not the solution at all.

What can you do?

If you can identify with one of these myths and realize that you or your organization are underprepared and at risk, seek some help. Succession planning by itself is not a difficult process – the decisions you might have to make can be extremely difficult. There are many qualified advisors who can help you develop a plan and walk you through the decision-making process, ensuring that you remain objective all the way. I can attest that it can be done. I have worked with dozens of organizations, public and private, for-profit and non-profit, large and small employee populations, to design and implement a succession planning process and subsequent plans that have been highly effective in protecting and growing the businesses.

A discussion about succession planning would be remiss if it did not include the topics of financial, tax and legal consequences of not having a well thought out plan. For those who have a significant financial stake in the company because of equity positions, addressing these technical issues is an important responsibility that is oftentimes overlooked. Be one of the organizations that plan to be around in the future by being prepared to face the future on your terms. Decide that you will influence how that happens and not be forced to react to a limited number of less than desirable options. Decide that you will not leave this responsibility to others in your family or business. Providing advice on these financial, tax and legal issues is beyond the scope of this book. Nevertheless, seek expert advice on these topics from qualified and godly professionals.

If you are a leader who has prayerfully developed and now implemented a succession plan and have turned over the reigns to your successor, the time is right for you to give up control of your former position – whether you are still with the organization or not. Follow the example of Moses who completely relinquished his responsibilities to Joshua.

If you are confident in the selection that was made and you are confident that God has made the selection, hanging around will only suggest that you are not so sure of the selection. Again, it might be well intentioned, but it can nevertheless signal that you doubt the right decision was made. This behavior is not helpful to the staff or to the new leader.

Finally, consider that the cost to provide leadership development will be far less than the money spent on replacing leaders who join other organizations that are more committed to developing their leaders. Research shows again and again that the cost of turnover of senior leaders can easily reach 150 to 200 percent of their base salary. That is quite expensive indeed. By investing five to ten percent of their base salary in annual leadership development initiatives, you will be investing wisely.

While providing opportunities and resources to continually develop leaders is not a fool-proof guarantee they will not leave, it does show that you value them enough to invest directly into their growth. This is worth a great deal. It might be enough for them to not return the call from a headhunter.

Leadership Development

With all that has been discussed to this point, a quote for reinforcement from a business leader hardly seems necessary, but the words spoken by Lee Iacocca are worth considering – "In the end, all business operations can be reduced to three words: people, product and profits. Unless you've got a good team, you can't do much with the other two." To have that "good team" you must have a strong, consistent and committed focus on developing leaders.

Leadership Lessons From THE BOOK

Self Assessment

Below are twenty statements that are indicative of a leader or an organization that has a sound leadership development process in place for building its current and future leaders. As you read the statements, be aware of the first response that comes to mind for you or the organization and circle the number in the appropriate column.

Never – 1	Seldom – 2	Sometimes – 3	Usually – 4	Always – 5

1. I am confident that God has appointed the leaders in this organization.

        1   2   3   4   5

2. I regularly pray before making any decision to select a new leader or promote someone into a leadership role.

        1   2   3   4   5

3. I practice the attitude of "the continual development of our leaders is directly connected with our ability to grow as an organization."

        1   2   3   4   5

4. I spend at least a third of my time on leadership development related work.

        1   2   3   4   5

5. Providing resources (time, focus and financial) for leadership development is one of the highest priority items we have in our annual operating plan and budget.

        1   2   3   4   5

6. Our organization invests in the tools and training for leadership development even at the expense of its profits.

        1   2   3   4   5

7. Our organization regularly reviews the leadership competencies established for this organization for continued importance and relevance.

   1   2   3   4   5

8. Our organization ensures that selection decisions for leadership positions are made considering a candidate's proficiency in our defined leadership competencies.

   1   2   3   4   5

9. Each of our key leaders has an individual development plan designed to enhance their leadership skills.

   1   2   3   4   5

10. The individual leadership development plans contain measurable goals and objectives.

   1   2   3   4   5

11. Our organization has a process to review progress of individual leadership development plans on a quarterly basis.

   1   2   3   4   5

12. Our organization has an up-to-date succession plan for each management-level position as well as key individual contributors.

   1   2   3   4   5

13. The succession plan has replacement candidates identified and has more than one replacement candidate for each position.

   1   2   3   4   5

14. Individuals with high potential to advance into leadership roles are identified in our organization.

   1   2   3   4   5

15. I fully appreciate that leadership development takes years, not weeks or months, to be accomplished.

       1   2   3   4   5

16. Our organization has a mentoring program in place and assesses its effectiveness on a regular basis.

       1   2   3   4   5

17. Each of the senior leaders has a mentor available to them other than me (or the top leader).

       1   2   3   4   5

18. Our organization utilizes a 360-degree feedback survey as an input source for leadership development initiatives.

       1   2   3   4   5

19. Our organization utilizes experiential learning as a leadership development tool.

       1   2   3   4   5

20. Our organization has developed strong relationships with outside advisors or vendors who can provide real value to our leadership development initiatives.

       1   2   3   4   5

Total your score here: _____

Leadership Development

If you scored between 80 and 100 – Congratulations, you (or your organization) have set and are executing a leadership development strategy with strength and purpose.

If you scored between 60 and 79 – You (or your organization) have made some great progress, yet have a way to go before truly having a long-term focus on leadership development.

If you scored under 60 – You (or your organization) are encouraged to take the necessary steps as outlined in this chapter to develop leadership development strategy for you and/or your organization that will enable the organization to have a competitive advantage and prepare leaders for future growth.

Practical Steps to Develop Leaders

Here are some practical steps for you to consider. As you read through and consider adopting some of these practices, take the opportunity to identify what you will eliminate from your current practice – if you need help in identifying what to eliminate, ask a trusted colleague, friend or advisor who is well versed in this critical aspect of leadership development.

1. Spend some time alone with God seeking His voice and direction on the leaders you have chosen to determine if those choices are aligned with His will for the organization at the current time. If you then determine that some inappropriate choices were made, resolve to take the necessary action.
2. Identify and clearly define eight to ten leadership competencies for your organization that are necessary for successful performance by anyone in a leadership role. If necessary, seek the help of an experienced consultant or advisor to guide you through this effort.
3. Conduct an objective assessment of the organization's leaders using a combination of reliable assessment tools, and have individualized leadership development plans created based on the results as well as the learning style of each leader.
4. Establish time in your calendar for a minimum quarterly review of the leadership development plan progress for each of your direct report leaders.
5. Identify leadership gaps within your organization in terms of specific leaders who need particular development in certain competency areas.
6. Identify vulnerability gaps your organization has in terms of lack of fully ready leaders available for key roles.
7. Develop and write a succession plan for key leadership positions in the organization, including the CEO position. Share the outcome with a trusted advisor who will be informed of your wishes and direction in case you are incapacitated in some way from implementing your plan.

8. Ensure the succession plan has at least one "ready-now" replacement for each key leadership role in the organization. If not, create actionable plans to achieve this within the next one or two years.
9. Ensure your succession plan is tied directly to your long-term strategic plan; you must have leaders capable of taking the organization where it plans to go.
10. Seek out a mentor or leadership coach to help you develop your commitment to developing leaders for the future.
11. Ensure each of your senior leaders has access to a mentor or executive coach.
12. Establish a budget for leadership development initiatives that equates to a particular percentage of revenue and commit to increase this percentage annually.
13. Consider implementing a 360-degree feedback survey for the leaders of the organization.
14. Initiate a process to identify and develop those with high potential to become the next generation leaders.
15. Schedule time in your calendar to speak to the organization on the importance of leadership development and back up your words with action.
16. Discuss the financial, tax and legal and consequences of the CEO succession plan with qualified advisors.

===
CHAPTER SIX
===

SETTING EXPECTATIONS

If you can not measure it, you can not manage it.

Scripture Passages

- "And the Lord God commanded the man saying, 'Of every tree of the garden you may freely eat; but of the tree of the knowledge of good and evil you shall not eat, for in the day that you eat of it you shall surely die.' " (Genesis 2:16-17 NKJV)
- "And on the eighth day he shall take two male lambs without blemish, one ewe lamb of the first year without blemish, three-tenths of an ephah of fine flour mixed with oil as a grain offering, and one log of oil." (Leviticus 14:10 NKJV)
- "And you shall love the Lord your God with all your heart, with all your soul, with all your mind, and with all your strength. You shall love your neighbor as yourself. There is no other commandment greater than these." (Mark 12:30-31 NKJV)
- "And He said to them, 'Take nothing for the journey, neither staffs nor bag nor bread nor money; and do not have two tunics apiece. Whatever house you enter, stay there, and from there depart. And whoever will not receive you, when you go out of that city, shake off the very dust from your feet as a testimony against them.' " (Luke 9:3-5 NKJV)

145

Leadership Lessons From THE BOOK

Introduction

Clear expectations are the starting point for effective performance. If we know what is expected and we commit to comply with those expectations, our performance will meet the standards of the one who set the expectations. If we do not know the expectations or the expectations are unclear, even if we wanted to comply, we would not be able to meet them.

In the introduction to the *Communication* chapter, I stated that most effective leaders spend considerable time thinking carefully about how, what and when to communicate. This is also true when setting and communicating expectations. Horst Schulze, the co-founder of the Ritz Carlton hotel chain is quoted as saying, "When someone makes the same mistake more than once, it is not a performance problem, it is problem with a procedure." What he means is that if the performance expectation or procedure is not crystal clear, it might cause people to make their interpretations which can lead to mistakes. Mistakes cost time and money which impacts our bottom line.

Quality focused organizations have adopted ISO standards and six sigma quality principles. In a manufacturing setting, these principles or operating standards are nothing more than setting clear expectations of performance for both equipment and personnel. The result has been that customers can trust the components or finished goods have been produced in accordance with strict standards. When this occurs, trust in the relationship between the manufacturer and the customer increases. Generally, with increased trust in the product or process comes increased business. The corollary to this is also quite true – when trust is decreased (because of expectations that are not delivered) less business is the outcome. The customer often seeks alternative suppliers or providers.

Additionally, clear expectations can reduce the need for rework or rechecking, all of which saves time and money, and results in higher profit margins. Generating higher profit margins means more can be invested in research, training and development of staff and leaders, giving back to God's Kingdom work and other worthy purposes. It just makes so much sense to set clear expectations. So why do organizations have so much trouble with this? Let us look at some lessons Scripture has about setting expectations.

Biblical Foundation

One of the first expectations God established and communicated to man had to do with what they could and could not eat. God communicated this expectation very clearly. Unfortunately for all of mankind, His expectation was not followed, and humans have been living with the consequences ever since. Actually, the expectation God communicated was a command and not an expectation. Therein could be the reason we have had such trouble through the centuries. Could it be that we, as humans, have come to believe that we are permitted to make our own interpretation of expectations that are placed on us? Adam and Eve certainly did with the help of the serpent.

Notice what happened as we read further in Genesis. Adam, the first leader of the human race, failed to stop Eve from eating the fruit. He was passive and allowed an incorrect interpretation of the expectation God had clearly communicated. Obviously God had (and will always have) the authority to establish an expectation. We run astray when we try to selectively interpret the expectation from our vantage point or perspective. We run astray when we rationalize that a particular expectation does not apply to us. We run astray when we think an expectation could be better carried out if we changed the such-and-such aspect of the expectation. We also run astray when we conform the expectation into what we desire rather than accommodate what is expected of us.

Adam made a feeble attempt at deflecting his responsibility as Eve's leader and blamed Eve for the sinful action. He even made an attempt at blaming God by referring to Eve as "the woman whom You gave to me." (Genesis 3:12) Blame has now been born as a technique for not accepting personal responsibility for our failure to comply with an expectation. When God confronted Eve, she tried to blame it on

Leadership Lessons From THE BOOK

the serpent. If both Adam and Eve had realized that God's clear expectation was to be followed and not to be interpreted, who knows what the human race would be like today?

Throughout the Bible, God has been crystal clear about the expectations He has set. Consider the following examples:

- The specific length, width and height of the ark were clearly stated to Noah. God also specified where the window and door were to be placed and how many levels the ark would contain. He even specified the material to be used (gopherwood and pitch), the animals to include and so on. (See Genesis 6)

- God instructed Joshua to have the people march around the walls of Jericho in silence once a day for six straight days and to walk around the wall seven times on the seventh day. On the seventh day, the priests were to blow trumpets, the people were to shout and the wall would collapse. We are confident that if the Israelites did not follow those expectations to the letter, the result would have been in vain. (See Joshua 6)

- The Israelites were defeated at Ai because one man, Achan, did not follow the clear expectations God established of not keeping any plunder from the previous battle. (See Joshua 7) Once the sin was confessed and dealt with, everyone else followed the clear expectations and victory over Ai was obtained, yet not before the Israelites were soundly defeated in their first attack.

- God set crystal clear expectations for King Saul in the battle with the Amalekites. Saul was to destroy them and everything they owned. Saul made his own interpretation of that expectation and decided to retain the best livestock. From that point on, God did not look favorably on Saul and removed the kingdom from him. (See I Samuel 15)

In the first two examples above, did you notice that when Noah and Joshua followed the expectations that God had communicated exactly, the outcome was what God had

148

promised them? Did you notice in the final two examples that when the expectations were not followed, or outright disobeyed, the outcomes were disastrous?

If we look at the instructions He gave to Joshua, the instructions seem a bit odd at first glance. After all, the people were dealing with the Almighty who forty years ago had parted the Red Sea immediately. He did not wait for seven days of marching around or horn blowing. The people were dealing with the Almighty who sent ten plagues and the angel of death without a lot of notice or preamble.

You can imagine what the conversation must have been like when Joshua outlined the expectations that God had given to him. You can imagine the Israelites forming some committees to discuss what Joshua said and providing suggestions to change the interpretation. That is certainly the approach we would take today. Yet we have a strong lesson provided for us to NOT interpret what we know to be instructions and expectations received from God – regardless of how odd they might sound. Isaiah 55:9 says, "for my ways are higher than your ways and my thoughts higher than your thoughts."

As we look at the specifics of the expectations that God has established, notice that He does not settle for second best. As He described His expectations for sacrifices in Leviticus, He was specific about the quality level. The animals were to be without blemish. Why? Simply because He wanted the Israelites to offer a real sacrifice, not an animal they would throw away anyway because of defects, blemishes, and broken bones. God wanted them to realize the actual penalty for sin. It required an animal of the best quality, without blemish or defect, to be sacrificed. Therefore, the cost to the sinner would be a higher cost as compared to an animal with a defect, which no one would want. God requires our best all the time and not just when it is convenient for us.

God was very specific in outlining the expectations He had for sacrifices. There were sin offerings, peace offerings, burnt offerings and freewill offerings. He was very specific in how lepers were to be treated. He was very specific on how the priests were to behave and what they were to wear. He was very specific as to the requirements for celebrating various feasts and holy days. Why was He so specific? He explained in Leviticus 15 that He was doing this so the people, who were naturally prone to sinning, would have an acceptable method of offering sacrifices to Him when they gathered near His Tabernacle. Since He is a holy God, He cannot accept people who have not been holy, so in His loving mercy He created standards for the people to comply with to be near His presence. If they did not follow these standards or expectations, they would die. Notice that God did not leave it to the Israelites to define or interpret what an acceptable method of sacrifice would be. He knew they (or we) would not measure up to His standards.

Man's interpretations of God's expectations are hardly ever accurate when we look at the requirement from our perspective. Even though we might not always comprehend the reason why God has established His expectations, it does not give us the authority to change them by interpreting them to our own satisfaction or justification. Do you think Adam, Noah, Achan or Saul knew the full purpose or intention of God's standards? Probably not.

Jesus helped us understand clear expectations God had for us by summing up the Law and the prophets when He responded to the scribe in Mark 12:30-31. Jesus said, in effect, to love God with all our heart, soul, mind and strength – that is pretty much all of our being. As a former pastor of mine was fond of saying, "All means all and that's all all means." Jesus went on to say that the second commandment was like it – to love our neighbor as we love ourselves.

What does He mean to love our neighbor as we love ourselves? As we consider how we would treat our own being, most relatively stable individuals would agree we would not harm, trick, manipulate, steal from, insult or ignore ourselves. This is the essence of the Golden Rule. Who is our neighbor? Our neighbor is the person or family who actually lives next door, in our neighborhood, in our community. Does this include those we work with, do business with, buy from, sell to and otherwise interact with? I think so. These are difficult expectations to live up to every day, without a doubt. However, the expectation is very clear.

If we do not have a commitment or attitude to follow the expectation, we immediately start off on the wrong foot. God knew that if we had any wiggle room to love Him less than He required, we would take it. He also knew that if we had any wiggle room in how we treated our neighbors, we would also take it. He knew that our pride and self-centeredness would have us focus on ourselves at the expense of our neighbors. We have proven that to Him for centuries so He commands us to live by a specific set of expectations.

When Jesus communicated His expectations to the twelve before He sent them out to preach, He was quite clear in what they should bring, how they should act and what they should do (preach the Kingdom of God and heal the sick). Some commentators say the reason Jesus told them not to bring staff, or bag, or money or bread was to focus on both the urgency of the situation and to rely on God's provision while they were doing His work. As leaders, before we communicate expectations, we must think about what is needed to successfully carry out the task.

Notice that Jesus even told them what to preach about (the Kingdom of God). Could He have left it up to them to decide the preaching topics? Sure, but chances are good that His purposes would not have been achieved, so He set clear expectations on what to preach. He told them to heal the sick; healing the sick created a buzz that got the attention of people. When their attention was captured, then the disciples could deliver the important, life-changing messages. When we follow the expectation and then experience the outcome, the reasons for the expectations become much clearer.

How great would it be if we as leaders would communicate our expectations to our staff as clearly as Jesus modeled? Some leaders do an extremely effective job at this, and we will discuss some the tools they use in this chapter.

151

Lessons Learned about Setting Expectations

1. Expectations are not to be interpreted by the ones who are to carry them out. They can only be modified by the leader who creates them.
2. Expectations are to be communicated in ways the intended audience is best able to clearly understand their exact meaning.
3. It is necessary to take the right amount of time to set clear expectations so the likelihood of misunderstanding is minimized.
4. When expectations are left for interpretation, expected performance will not be achieved.

Practical Application

As God's Word has shown us, setting expectations is nothing more than being clear about what is expected. To be effective, leaders must be clear in the expectations and standards they set for the performance of those whose work they direct. There are a variety of tools available for leaders to set expectations.

Core Values

It all must begin with the core values that are established for an organization. Core values are those principles of behavior that are expected to be followed by every staff member. The core values God established regarding how we are to love Him and our neighbors are the bedrock for all the other expectations He has communicated. If we are committed Christians, it stands to reason that the core values for a Christian-based organization most definitely must include honoring God and following biblical principles.

Core values are what an organization is built on. Whereas the vision and mission are statements of intent and purpose, core values are statements of *how* the intent will be carried out; they are statements of how the organization will behave in carrying out the vision and mission. They are foundational.

The core values of the R.W. Beckett Corporation are stated as follows:

> R.W. Beckett is built on a platform of three core values: integrity, excellence and profound respect for the individual. Beckett works to nurture relationships daily: with our employees by creating a work environment that fosters growth and well-being; with our customers by providing products that are well-made, priced fairly and supported technically; and with our suppliers and others with whom we conduct business by treating them as we would like to be treated. We strive to serve the "larger good," helping meet human needs in the community and beyond.

> The character of a company is determined by those in leadership — their values, their competence, their commitment, their ability to work well together, and the example they set. We aspire to the finest possible management at all levels, seeking long-term relationships, internal and external, based on respect and trust.

> Our company endeavors to apply a biblically-based philosophy throughout every phase of its operations, providing a corporate atmosphere that promotes individual health, advancement in learning and strong families.

Organizations might say one thing, yet enable or allow their executives or staff to act a different way. For example, suppose the CEO proclaims that the organization will display the utmost honesty and integrity possible. How realistic is this expectation if the sales or customer service department still tells white lies to the customers about the status of the shipment to cover up for an error in placing the order? What if the accounts payable department continues to tell vendors "the check is in the mail" when they are instructed to hold onto the check to earn the interest float? What if a church organization who preaches about the love of Christ treats its employees in a disrespectful manner?

As long as these behaviors are allowed to continue, how will employees believe management is serious about a culture with high honesty and integrity? At the very best, they will believe that integrity is something to strive for, yet there is a lot of room for interpretation. We have seen earlier in the Biblical Foundation section how our own interpretation can cause a lot of trouble. As the Bible states, if we can not be trusted with the little things, God will not trust us with the bigger things. Exemplifying the core values all of the time is one of those requirements that God expects of us as Christian leaders.

In the *Business By The Book Workshop* by Larry Burkett, Howard Dayton and David Rae, it is suggested that the core values be documented. This helps to:

- Clarify God's mission for the organization
- Maintain focus on the manner in which God wants you to perform
- Promote unity in the organization and help new members understand its culture.

Ensuring new hires can operate within the core values is important. It is a good practice to identify a candidate's core values during the employee selection process. Conducting cultural fit assessments of candidates for employment is a small price to pay to save hundreds of thousands of dollars in replacement or poor decision costs.

This can be accomplished using a variety of techniques starting from simple behavioral interviewing to highly predictive (and somewhat costly) psychological assessments. In the middle are surveys that candidates can take to describe their style that can be overlaid onto an organization's core value patterns. Additionally, utilizing behaviorally-based interview techniques reveals exactly how a candidate has behaved, responded or acted in prior situations. Past behavior is the best predictor of future behavior.

Skipping this step allows for the potential of hiring employees and other leaders who do not operate within the core values. This creates an inconsistent message being sent to other employees, customers, suppliers and others. This will lead to a gradual eroding of the values to the point where they will be followed if it is convenient or profitable and will be ignored if there is another way to make a profit or accomplish what is considered to be a key goal.

When Jesus observed the Pharisees saying one thing (the core values) and practicing something different, He called them hypocrites. He said that we could identify the people's values based on their actions (see Matthew 7:20).

Job Descriptions

Samuel might have been the first to write a job description. Consider this verse from I Samuel 10:25 (NLT), "Then Samuel told the people what the rights and duties of a king were. He wrote them down on a scroll and placed it before the Lord." This verse comes as Samuel was anointing Saul to be Israel's first king. We know from reading Samuel that he would not do anything the Lord did not first instruct him to do. Clarifying the rights and duties of a position, even the position of king, was an appropriate thing to do, and Samuel did it.

Job descriptions are a useful tool that can provide a broad outline of duties a person is responsible for performing. Effective and useful job descriptions list ten or more key job duties or responsibilities along with performance measures that will be used to assess actual results. Comprehensive job descriptions also include position requirements detailing the skills and experience needed. They also contain detailed descriptions of competencies necessary for successful performance. See the discussion in the *Leadership Development* Chapter about competencies.

Job descriptions and the elements mentioned above are helpful when assessing candidates for open positions.

Unfortunately, one of the most common mistakes in the hiring process occurs when the multiple individuals involved in making the hiring decision do not discuss or formally agree to what they believe is needed by the person filling the position. In other words, their expectations are different. Detailed job descriptions and agreeing on those requirements before the first candidate is interviewed can help alleviate this costly error.

Knowing the experience and knowledge requirements necessary for successful performance is important. Equally important is to know the personality characteristics that are necessary for successful performance. For example, would it be prudent to hire a person who was not detail oriented into an accounting role? Would it be prudent to hire an extremely introverted person or a person with low self-confidence into an outside sales position? Matching the personality or trait requirements to a job is a necessary step in hiring the right person, and using valid and predictable personality assessment tools is a small investment to make that will have significant returns.

Performance Expectations

A suggested method of defining performance expectations starts by identifying each and every task the job is required to perform. With each task identified, define the quantifiable measures of performance that will be used in assessing actual performance. This might be somewhat tedious in the beginning. However, clients have agreed it is well worth the effort to ensure clear and consistent expectations are developed and communicated. This method has worked for years in manufacturing when establishing quality and quantity requirements. It is often resisted when applying it to people performing jobs. We need to stop resisting. God applied it to us, so why would we not apply it to us?

The old adage, "if you can not measure it, you can not manage it", comes to mind. How can you possibly train, coach or manage the employee expected to deliver an outcome if you can not objectively and quantifiably measure the expected outcome of a task you expect to be accomplished? How do you assess their performance in an objective manner? Unfortunately there are still managers and leaders who utilize the "I will know good performance when I see it" approach. This approach is a shot in the dark. Without having a quantifiable system or process to measure output, performance can not be accurately assessed. In Genesis 6, God knew how long it would take Noah to fully construct the ark. He also provided Noah with the specifications that would be exactly appropriate for His purposes.

Establishing performance expectations requires that each and every task, down to the simplest one, has a measurable outcome attached to its performance. If the task cannot be measured as such, try to restate the task so it can be measured. God did not tell the Israelites to just offer Him sacrifices; He gave them specific expectations as to when to offer them, for what reason and what was to be considered acceptable as a sacrifice. He did not tell Noah to just build an ark. He provided specific instructions to be followed and was precise about the measurements, locations of doors and windows and provisions to be stored.

We conduct studies and analyses to determine the exact output a particular machine should produce in a given amount of time. We identify the amount of raw materials that are necessary to produce the widget. We identify the amount of waste or scrap that is acceptable, and we identify the quality levels that are expected. We use this information to price the cost to produce these widgets, adding on labor cost, overhead and profit. We have performance expectations for the machines we utilize, why not for people performing particular tasks? Establishing performance expectations for people will significantly improve efficiency and add to the bottom line. It will also enable a stronger focus on specific hiring criteria as well as training needs.

If we truly believe God laid out performance expectations for those who desire to follow Him, reflect on what Proverbs 30:5-6 says, "Every word of God is flawless; he is a shield to those who take refuge in him. Do not add to his words, or he will rebuke you and prove you a liar." These are some pretty strong affirming words about the validity of God's Word as well as what happens when people make an attempt to misinterpret or misapply His instruction or His performance expectations.

SMART Goals

As discussed in the *Setting A Vision* chapter, SMART goals are an effective tool to set and measure goals, which in turn establish expectations. A goal is defined as follows: A written statement that clearly describes certain actions or tasks with a measurable end result. SMART is an acronym for **S**pecific, **M**easureable, **A**chievable, **R**elevant, and **T**ime-bound. *Specific* goals are actions or tasks that are exact, precise and detailed. *Measureable* goals have quantifiable results in mind so that the actions can be tied to a particular outcome. Increasing sales of X product by 10 percent is both specific and measurable. *Achievable* goals are those actions which are realistic. They are not so easy that they require little to no effort nor are they so difficult that they are impossible to reach. *Relevant* goals are actions and tasks that can be directly connected to the furtherance of the mission and purpose of the organization. To work on a goal that is not relevant to the organizational purpose is not worth investing time or money. Finally, *Time-bound* goals establish a target completion date.

To have a goal that says "increase sales" is not a SMART goal. Restated as a SMART goal, it might read, "Increase unit sales of x product by 10 percent over last year's actual unit sales by the end of the fourth quarter." Goals that are not SMART in their description generally lead to disappointing results because clear expectations for the outcome were not established, communicated or understood.

Policies and Procedures

Standard operating procedures, employee handbooks and human resource or personnel policies are all examples of other tools to establish and communicate requirements that employees are expected follow. When you board a plane to take a trip somewhere, it is comforting to know that the pilot and cockpit crew have a written and very specific set of pre-flight procedures they must follow before they even start the engine and pull away from the gate. Is it not reassuring to know that the flight attendants have a standard set of procedures to perform in the cabin prior to taxiing down the runway?

Like core values, policies and procedures are written expectations that organizations use to guide the performance and behavior of the employees. Without them, companies might be tempted to scale back on the most costly ingredient of their product in order to make another penny or two in the sale price.

Typically, as leaders, the more employees we have under our direction, the less likely we are able to watch over each one all the time (nor is it appropriate leadership behavior to constantly watch over employees under our authority). Clearly stated policies and procedures are an effective aid to ensure employees perform certain repetitive tasks and behaviors in a manner that will produce predictable results – results leading to successful performance.

Policies and procedures must be aligned with the core values of the organization. If not, employees will be forced to choose between one or the other, and then we run the risk of allowing for individual interpretation. We know where that will lead. The overall message here is that expectations must be crystal clear and not subject to interpretation. We know all too well the result when Adam and Eve or King Saul thought they were allowed to interpret one of God's clear expectations.

Practical Steps to Exhibit in Setting Expectations

1. Have a group (task force or committee) review policies, procedures and handbooks to assess if they are crystal clear in the stated expectations.
2. Prepare clear and measurable performance expectations for every key task of the positions reporting directly to you and ask the person performing the job to comment on the expectations.
3. If needed, restate key tasks in a manner that each can have at least one measurable performance expectation attached to it. If you can not measure it, you can not manage it or expect a performance standard to be achieved.
4. Consider establishing SMART goals for each direct report and holding monthly progress meetings with each person.
5. Develop or update the core values; ensure all staff members are fully aware of them.
6. Evaluate performance expectations, policies, procedures and handbooks against the organization's core values to ensure consistency.
7. Look for and correct opportunities that staff might have to interpret expectations, policies or procedures.
8. Evaluate and improve the hiring process to ensure that candidates are assessed against the core values of the organization. Talk to leaders in other organizations or knowledgeable consultants about reliable assessment tools.
9. Improve the hiring process by ensuring that each person who has input into the selection of the final candidate has the same understanding of the job requirements, experiences and competencies needed before anyone meets with a candidate.
10. Create a task item on your calendar to provide some kind of performance feedback to each member of your staff at least once each week.
11. Evaluate the tasks most prone to errors, mistakes or rework and reassess the stated performance expectations. Tighten and clarify those expectations as necessary.

12. Ensure accurate and up-to-date job descriptions exist for each position reporting to you.
13. Enhance the value of existing job descriptions by having clearly defined competencies for each position.
14. Ensure you and your boss are in complete alignment with the expectations he or she has for your performance.
15. Identify instances where behaviors seem to be inconsistent with the stated or intended core values. Take appropriate steps to correct the behavior immediately and inform the staff of the expected changes.
16. Identify any staff member who has demonstrated an unwillingness to conform to any of the core values and provide appropriate opportunities for that person to leave the organization, including involuntary separation if necessary.
17. As you define and communicate new expectations, ask a staff member to repeat or paraphrase their understanding of the expectation to ensure complete clarity.
18. Evaluate stated expectations from the viewpoint of the intended audience. Are you sure they understand what is being asked of them?
19. Whenever possible, avoid the use of jargon in the definition of competencies or expectations.
20. Evaluate stated expectations from a biblical standpoint – are they in line with what you know to be God's expectations?

==
CHAPTER SEVEN
==

STEWARDSHIP

God owns it all, including your organization

Scripture Passages

- "The earth is the Lord's, and everything in it. The world and all its people belong to him." (Psalm 24:1 NLT)
- "Everything in the heavens and on earth is yours O Lord, and this is your kingdom. We adore you as the one who is over all things." (I Chronicles 29:11 NLT)
- "The master was full of praise. 'Well done my good and faithful servant. You have been faithful in handling this small amount, so now I will give you many more responsibilities. Let's celebrate together.' " (Matthew 25:21 NLT)

Introduction

Webster defines steward as "a person put in charge of a large estate" or "an administrator, as of finances or property." Wikipedia suggests that a steward is "a servant who manages property." Another definition from Wikipedia defines a steward as "a person who manages the property or affairs for another entity."

Today, with pension plans, 401(K)s and other retirement savings options, we typically turn over the management of those funds to a financial manager. This person is a steward in that they manage money for someone else. The financial manager does not own the assets or the money. They just manage it for someone else, carrying out the owner's wishes for returns. The financial manager has the responsibility and accountability to safeguard and manage these funds by following particular rules and regulations and for making decisions that are in the best interest of the owner.

Landlords will sometimes hire a building manager who will be responsible for the day-to-day management of their buildings, ensuring that various repairs and maintenance chores are taken care of so the tenants are able to live comfortably. The building manager is not the owner, yet he or she is accountable for managing the asset on behalf of the owner and for making decisions that are in the owner's best interest.

Even as Christians, we might forget that God owns everything, and we are merely stewards or managers of what He entrusts to us. Yes, He is the Lord who provides, and sometimes we forget why He provides what He does. Romans 8:28 tells us that all things work together for good for those who love God, to those who are called according to His purpose. In this passage, all things include all provisions working together for good. For us to be faithful stewards we must manage what God has provided to us in a manner that achieves His purposes, not ours. We need to put *His* purposes ahead of ours.

There are people who struggle with the concept of God owning everything. For many of these people, I suspect that they make decisions based on how that decision will impact

Stewardship

them or those closest to them. As for stewards, we make decisions based on what we humbly believe God wants us to do for His purposes, not ours. Matthew 6:33 instructs us to seek first the Kingdom of God and His righteousness. This means that in all our thoughts, behaviors, actions and decisions, we must put the Kingdom of God first before ourselves.

Where has God called us to be stewards of what He owns? Let's find out what His word says about the topic of stewardship.

Biblical Foundation

God clearly established from the beginning that He, the creator of the world and everything in it, owns it all. When God instructed the Israelites through Moses, He commanded that the land should not be sold permanently, for this land is His (Leviticus 23:23). In Deuteronomy 10, Moses recalls when God called him to bring two new tablets up the mountain so the Ten Commandments could again be written on the tablets. When he came back down from the mountain, he told Israel what the Lord required of them. In verse 12, Moses said the essence of the law was to fear the Lord, to walk in all His ways, to love Him, to serve Him with all your heart and soul, and to keep the commandments and statues of the Lord. In verse 14, Moses reminded the Israelites that the earth and everything in it belongs to God. God also reminded Job that everything under heaven was His (Job 41:11).

God has always intended for the human race to be stewards or managers of what is His. Genesis 2:15 (NKJV) says, "Then the Lord God took the man and put him in the Garden of Eden to tend and keep it." Notice that God did not transfer ownership to the man; He just transferred the responsibility to manage the garden. Our sovereign God has had the clear distinction between ownership and stewardship in mind from the beginning. God gave us examples to follow as Joseph was the overseer of Potiphar's house. Do not miss this – Potiphar saw that the Lord was with Joseph and that is why

165

Potiphar appointed Joseph as the overseer or steward (see Genesis 39:1-6). A few years later, Pharaoh himself recognized that Joseph was a man of God. He referred to Joseph as "a man in whom is the Spirit of God" (Genesis 41:38 NKJV) and then made Joseph the governor over the entire land.

In Psalm 24, the psalmist David recognized that God owns it all. He recognized that since God is the Creator and He established everything that anyone on the Earth could see, therefore all belongs to Him. Since God owns it all, all aspects of our lives must come under His authority. It is as Paul asks in Romans 9:20-21, "who are we, the clay, to say to the potter (the Creator) why have you made me like this?" God also made it clear to Job when He asked, "Where were you when I laid the foundation of the earth?" (Job 38:4 NKJV) The entire series of questions that God asks Job in chapters 38 and 39 as well as the challenges God gives Job in chapters 40 and 41 would make anyone shudder to the awesomeness and power of the Almighty.

Recall the interpretation of the word "all" I mentioned earlier from a former pastor. He said, "All means all and that's all all means." In this context, all certainly means all, and God owns it all.

Since God was the one to make it all, and He is sovereign in all, He makes it quite clear that He is the rightful owner of everything. Even though God owns it all and all people should acknowledge this fact, David is saying that as God's chosen people, they must behave differently than the others who did not believe that God really existed. Otherwise, if the Israelites did not behave differently, by knowing that the God of the Israelites was the one and true God, what would cause the other nations to alter their behavior or have a desire to learn about God? The same can be said of us as Christians. God has set us apart, so we need to behave as though we have been set apart. One of those behaviors is to acknowledge that God does own it all and we are stewards.

David wanted the Israelites to understand the responsibility they had to serve the King who created it all and owned it all. In demonstrating this respectful and holy behavior, other nations might take notice. David also wanted to remind the people of their responsibility to regularly acknowledge God and His sovereignty over all things.

In Psalm 24, David asks a question, "Who may stand in His holy place?" (24:3) and answers this question by stating, "only those with clean hands and a pure heart." Clean hands and a pure heart refer to the actions, behaviors, motives and intentions of the person who desires to serve God. The clean hands refers to the actions and behaviors whereas the pure heart refers to the motives and intentions. David is extolling the Israelites that their work and their motives must respect God's holiness because, as creator and owner of it all, He deserves nothing less.

Psalm 50 is full of references to God owning it all. Consider the following verses from the NIV:

- "The Mighty One, God, the Lord, speaks and summons the earth from the rising of the sun to the place where it sets" (v 1). (Who could rightfully summon something they do not own?)
- "He summons the heavens above, and the earth, that he may judge his people" (v 4).
- "I have no need of a bull from your stall or of goats from your pens, for every animal of the forest is mine and the cattle on a thousand hills" (v 9-10).
- "I know every bird in the mountains and the creatures of the field are mine" (v 11).
- "If I were hungry I would not tell you, for the world is mine and all that is in it" (v 12).

These verses make is so clear that God owns it all. He is in charge, and we are not. Additionally, Proverbs 15:3 (NLT) says, "The Lord is watching everywhere, keeping his eye on both the evil and the good." The little word "is" provides us with hope and assurance that our sovereign God is always aware and therefore allowing *all* things that actually happen to happen. There is not one thing, event or occurrence that surprises Him or takes Him off guard. The word everywhere means all places –

there is not a place on earth or the universe where He is not aware of what is going on. And we can not forget what Hanani the seer told Asa the king of Judah, in II Chronicles 16:9, which certainly still applies today, "For the eyes of the Lord range throughout the earth to strengthen those whose hearts are fully committed to him."

In I Chronicles 29, David has just finished gathering all the materials that he and the leaders of Israel had donated to build the Temple. Note that they appeared to be cheerful givers because they recognize that God owns it all and in His loving kindness, provided many blessings upon them. In this verse, David is blessing the Lord in front of the entire assembly by remembering that all that is in heaven and on earth is His and that He is to be exalted as head over all things. In verse 12, he says that both riches and honor come from God and He reigns over all. He continues on in his prayer to thank God. In verses 16-17, David recognizes that all this giving has to come from an "uprightness of heart" and a willingness to give.

Here again, we see that David is providing us with the criteria for acting, much like the clean hands and pure heart mentioned in Psalm 24. God requires that we have our behaviors and intentions aligned for His purposes. David and the people have recognized that God has provided for them for a reason – to provide back to Him what was needed to build the Temple which was being built to honor Him.

Since David acknowledges that God is the source and owner of it all, no doubt he has told this to the people throughout his time as Israel's king. He reminds the people that God is the provider. God is responsible for the riches they have received. David is proud that the people would realize their responsibility for discerning how God wanted those resources He provided to be used and that they would willingly give of those resources to honor God.

In His wisdom and providence, God has also provided a few lessons of poor or ineffective stewardship from which we can learn much. The priest Eli had two sons, Hophni and Phinehas. They were not good stewards. They are described as corrupt and greedy, and they did not follow the prescribed laws for priests, but took for themselves what they wanted. God knew about their behavior. He chastised Eli for not taking the appropriate action and God caused the death of the two sons. See I Samuel 2.

Another lesson in poor stewardship is King Saul. He thought he could be exempt from doing what God instructed him to do. In I Samuel 13, we read that Saul was overly influenced by the opinions of his military men when they were discouraged after one of their many battles with the Philistines. Despite God's clearly communicated instructions to His steward Saul through Samuel, Saul decided that he could not wait for Samuel to arrive and conducted the sacrifice. Even though Saul was using the offering to ask for God's blessing before going into battle, he did not follow the timing instructions Samuel had so clearly stated. Samuel's response found in verse 13 essentially called Saul a fool. He admonished Saul for not keeping the command the Lord had given, and as a result, this action would cost Saul the kingdom. Saul was not a good steward of what God had asked him to manage.

When God is displeased with those who are supposed to be stewards, He takes away the privilege and the responsibility of being a steward and gives it to someone else. In the case of Eli's two sons, who would have taken over as the priests after Eli died, God appointed Samuel instead. When King Saul could not effectively handle the responsibility, God appointed David to be King. As Romans 8:28 promises, the good that came out of these situations were Samuel and David, two of Israel's finest leaders.

Psalm 37:4 says we are to delight ourselves in the Lord, and He will give us the desires of our heart. To delight ourselves in the Lord means that we work diligently to know and understand the things that are most important to God's heart. Does that include our organization? Yes, most definitely. To know what is important to God's heart, we must try our best to see it from His perspective. Part of what God's heart desires is for His name to be exalted and His Kingdom to be further extended. Can we do this in our organization? Most assuredly, for this is what He calls us to do. Our priorities and His priorities must be aligned, and this can only happen when we seek to know and understand the priorities that are most important to Him.

By the way, the responsibilities, to exalt His name and to extend His Kingdom, are not reserved for the church or missionaries. As we will discuss, God provides each one of us with a set of skills, abilities and talents to carry out this work where He has placed us. As leaders of all kinds of organizations, we are called to be salt and light in and to a world full of darkness.

Jesus tells us a parable in Matthew commonly referred to as the Parable of the Talents. You likely know the parable well. In this parable, as the master was preparing to leave for a long journey, he called three of his servants and gave each a sum of money. We are clearly instructed to view this term of 'talents' as not just money. We are to include all of what God has provided to us in terms of time, skills and abilities as well as our money.

The master clearly expected the three slaves to be stewards of what he was about to transfer to them. He expected each one to manage the money they were provided on his behalf while he was away. As we learn, his expectation was for the servants to not merely protect the money, but to take some action that would result in the master making money, even if it just earned interest from a banker. We can also reasonably discern that the master provided three different sums to each of the slaves based on what the master determined they could handle. The slave who was given the five talents was deemed to be better skilled than the slave who was given the one talent. God does not give us more than what He has gifted us to handle.

Jesus tells us that after being away for a long time, the master returned. Jesus was referring to the time it would take between His first and second comings. He clearly tells us that He will evaluate what we as His stewards have accomplished with what He has provided. He will assess what we did with His possessions. He expects some significant gains.

When the master returned, he was full of praise for the first servant, for having doubled his money. The master was not only pleased, he was impressed with the slave's actions, so much so that he gave the slave what seemed to be a significant promotion. In Luke's version of this parable found in Chapter 19, we are told the master gave the first servant "authority over ten cities" because he was faithful in such a little assignment. The second slave received praise as well for the action he took and was rewarded in a manner commensurate with his results. The third slave was chastised because all he did was hide the money.

The third slave might have been self-centered. Perhaps he did not agree with the master's way of doing business. It was this slave who commented that the master would reap where he did not sow. Maybe it was his way of rebelling against the master. In any event, he did not perform in a manner that the master had expected. After all, he did nothing with the talent he was given except bury it. He did not use it to advance his master's wealth. He knew the master was a harsh man, yet he chose to do nothing. He did not even think to place it with a banker to gain a little interest. This slave might have confidently thought he knew best how to use the talent he was asked to manage. He was therefore punished for doing his own thing and not looking after the best interest of his master.

In the end, this last slave was stripped of everything. The lesson here is that the leader who does not work at being a good steward will be judged and punished for his or her failure to recognize the real Owner of their business, their talents and their life. For we know that God rewards those who are faithful to Him, and He punishes those who are not. God requires faithfulness in all things, including your role as a leader.

To be good stewards, we must seek God's will in what He would have us do with what He has entrusted us to manage for Him. In John 15, Jesus tells us that we must abide or remain in Him, for apart from Him, we can not accomplish anything of value. Therefore, we must understand what He wants us to do with what He has entrusted us to manage. God is not asking us to perform a function because He cannot perform that function. He is asking us to perform a function to see how we will respond. He wants to know if we will be faithful with what we

171

have been given to manage. He wants to know whether we can be trusted with little before He can trust us with more. If we can not be trusted to effectively steward or manage a little, He will not abandon us, but He will not give us more than we can be trusted to effectively manage.

To separate or segregate what we are doing as leaders from the will and purpose of Almighty God is actually putting our needs before His perfect desires. We are showing God that we are more concerned about our priorities and plans rather than His. As senior pastors, executive directors, or CEOs, we would never act against the wishes of our board. Doing so would clearly and appropriately result in our removal from the position. Why should it be any different when we consider our relationship with God as a steward over what He has called us to lead?

We are called to stay in touch with the Owner of it all, and to know what His intentions and purposes are and for us to carry them out. When we acknowledge this, God is faithful and will give us the tools, talents, strength and staff to carry this out for His purposes and His glory. When you think about it seriously, there really is no other way to operate as a leader.

Lessons Learned about Stewardship

1. God owns it all, including your organization.
2. Our actions and motives as a steward must be respectful of God's purposes and His holiness.
3. Our priorities must be aligned with God's priorities.
4. We must be in constant touch with God to fully understand His purposes, direction and priorities.
5. God will test us with a little responsibility before allowing us to have a greater responsibility.

Stewardship

Practical Application

When we acknowledge that God owns it all, our approach to decision making changes. It changes from making decisions that impact us or people close to us to making decisions as a manager of someone else's organization – in their best interest, not ours. This is a huge shift in thinking. We can no longer make impulsive decisions based on opportunities that come our way. We have to put those opportunities in the context of the organization being God's organization, and seek to know what He, as the owner, would have us do. We become less self-centered and more God-centered. He desires for us to behave in this manner.

When faced with decisions to go after particular opportunities, we must now take into account that we are stewards of an organization. What does the Owner want us to do? Does the Owner want us to incur debt in order that we might buy machinery, land, building or whatever in order to take advantage of the opportunity? Does the Owner want us to pay interest on that debt when that same amount of money could be going to fund Kingdom advancement initiatives?

If we have been provided with a new customer who will substantially increase our revenue and net profit, what do we do with the new funds? Does the Owner want us to buy brand new office furniture or the latest computer equipment? Or does He want us to use the money to develop future leaders or offer scholarships so our employees' children attend a Christian summer camp?

These are hard questions indeed, especially if we follow the secular world's guidance on how to spend money and make decisions. Yet, if we follow biblical principles and act as stewards, the answers, although sometimes difficult to implement, will become easier to make. As a friend of mine says, "Decisions are made easy when you know what you stand for."

If we truly believe that God owns it all, then the next natural action is to place all of our leadership thoughts, beliefs, actions and decisions under His lordship. (After all, we sing this

173

during the hymn, "I Surrender All"!) This changes how we think and how we act because we now act as stewards or managers and not as owners. We want to act in a manner that will have our Lord and Savior say, "Well done, good and faithful servant" when we see Him.

Proverbs 16:2 says, "All a man's ways seem innocent to him, but motives are weighed by the Lord." It is not about our standards, it is about the Lord's standards. As a leader who runs an organization, we might be running it in a way that is pure in our own eyes. However, we must ask if this is the standard God has in mind for us as His appointed stewards.

Being a steward requires a change in our attitude from that of an owner to that of a manager. We are required to subordinate our own desires and wishes to those of the true Owner. We are charged with carrying out His plans, not ours. We are now responsible – and will be held accountable – for fully understanding what the Owner wants to accomplish and to subordinate what we think is best to accomplish. We are accountable for understanding what the Owner's long-term plans are for the organization He has called us to manage. This puts quite a different spin on what we do, does it not?

In the accounts described in I Kings 13 and 14, the Lord made it clear to the kings at the time that He would bless them if they kept His commands. In other words, if they acted as a steward of what God owns, He would be honored and they would receive blessings. It seemed easy enough. Yet, they disobeyed, primarily by worshipping idols and other gods. John tells us that some of the Jewish leaders in Jesus' day believed in Jesus but would not admit it for fear of the Pharisees who would expel them from the synagogue. John 12:43 (NLT) says, "For they loved human praise more than praise from God."

Perhaps the kings suffered from the same disease as the Jewish leaders – loving human praise more than praise from God. They preferred answering the call of what the people wanted them to do (building pagan shrines, idols, unsacred altars, etc.) than what God wanted them to do. In both accounts, how foolish they were to pick the praise of people over the praise of God. How about Christian leaders today? What does our behavior show about whose praise is more important to us? What does our behavior show about whose priorities are more important to us? We have to be aware of how we answer this as other people are watching what we do. God is also very aware of how we answer these questions and uses this information to decide if we can be trusted with more.

We will be held accountable for decisions we make concerning the treatment of those employees who are under our supervision. Did we treat them fairly and with respect? Did we compensate them appropriately so they could provide for their family? Have we developed them to be the best they could be, not for our gain, but for God's gain? Did we offer them opportunities to know the Lord and grow their relationship with Him? In a similar way, we will be held accountable for how we treat our customers, our vendors and suppliers and well as those in our community.

This is one of the reasons it is so important to be part of a Christian leader's accountability group. We need to be an active member of a forum of like-minded leaders where we can bounce ideas and obtain advice. For businesses, Fellowship of Companies for Christ International (www.fcci.org) is just such an organization. Another fine organization is C12 Group (www.C12Group.com). Being part of a group like this will help you discern what God's plans are for His organization.

Proverbs 13:20 (NLT) says, "Walk with the wise and become wise, associate with fools and get in trouble." Proverbs 19:20 (NLT) says, "Get all the advice and instruction you can, so you will be wise the rest of your life." Proverbs 19:27 (NLT) says, "If you stop listening to instruction my child, you will turn your back on knowledge." The common theme here is to always be looking for wise counsel, instruction and advice. We are to seek this from godly people and godly leaders. If we rely on obtaining advice from fools or from ungodly leaders, Scripture says we will get in trouble, we will lose focus on leading by God's way and we will be much more susceptible to following the advice the world has to offer. We know from Proverbs 2 that following worldly advice will move us onto the path the wicked and evil walk.

Proverbs 15:14 (NLT) says, "A wise person is hungry for knowledge, while the fool feeds on trash." Here again, we are given good advice as to where to seek the knowledge and counsel we need to be godly leaders. If we rely on the secular world for such advice, it is equivalent to feeding on trash because the secular world has no intention of honoring God. The secular world is about short-term, temporal gain and personal pleasure. As stewards of God's organizations, we must be focused on longer-term, eternal, kingdom purposes.

We must also have regular time with God alone in prayer and reflection. Many people spend a great deal of time developing plans for their organization, and then submitting those plans to God for His blessing. According to Scripture, this approach is backward. We should first spend time alone with God, allow Him to reveal to us His plans and purposes and then use the talents He has given us to initiate and implement specific actions that will bring His plans to fruition. One might say, "If I do it that way, I will miss a great opportunity." I would respond, "If you do not do it that way, you will *definitely* miss a *greater* opportunity." If we desire to have God trust us with more then we must follow His way.

As leaders, we have a difficult time with the concept of subordinating our desires to another. This is especially true for founders of organizations. As leaders, we believe people are counting on us to provide vision and direction. This is true. The difficult act of subordinating our desires is exactly what God is calling us to do. When we subordinate our desires for God's plans and purposes, we become the messenger or the facilitator to communicate and enable God's purposes to be accomplished through our management.

Psalm 84:11b (NLT) says, "The Lord will withhold no good thing from those who do what is right." If we focus on what God desires, on His priorities and do what is right, our priorities and His priorities will be aligned. As a steward, we have to be aligned with the Owner's priorities, otherwise, we are not performing as the Owner desires, and He will find another person to steward the organization. Remember what happened to Eli and to King Saul? As we align our priorities together with

His, we will begin to see what God sees and see the needs as God sees them. If He desires to do a work through us, He will provide all we need to accomplish that work. That is great! We do not have to worry about where the resources will come from or how we will accomplish it. It is God's job, and He has proven to be quite the provider. The first step, however, is to ensure our priorities are aligned with His. We do this by abiding in Him.

As stewards, we must determine what God wants to do with the organization He has chosen for us to lead. If you are in doubt as to what God has asked you to do, commit to spend more time in His word, and with other godly people who can guide you. Also, review the *Setting A Vision* chapter in this book again.

Proverbs 15:26 (NLT) says, "The Lord detests evil plans." This is similar to the rebuke Jesus gave to the Pharisees in Luke 16:15b (NLT) when He said, "What this world honors is detestable in the sight of God." Do we want our plans, behaviors and values to be evil by not allowing God to formulate them? Do we want to honor what the world honors when we know it is detestable to God? We must set our plans according to what God wants us to do as stewards of His provision.

The book of Judges uses a phrase again and again: "The people did whatever seemed right in their own eyes." This phrase meant the people had strayed away from following God's commands and followed their own desires. This typically led to idol worship, inter-marrying and similar sins against God. God would then allow one of their enemies to capture them and rule them for a while. The people would once again realize why they were in the predicament they were in and repent of their sin. In His mercy, God would raise up a judge to bring the people back into fellowship with Him. This would last for awhile and then (guess what?) the people would stray again. It was a vicious cycle.

When we run our organizations without following God's principles, we are guilty of doing the same thing the Israelites did thousands of years ago. When we follow the world's standards, we are in effect doing whatever seems right in our own eyes. Companies see a great opportunity to grow their business, and they hire a bunch of people to make it happen. Then some other company comes along and figures out a way to do it better and takes market share away from the original company. The original company ignores the signs until the only recourse is to lay off people in order to survive. We have seen this pattern occur time and time again. We are doing what seems to be right in our own eyes.

Does this behavior honor God? Is this the behavior God wants us to exhibit as His steward and representative running His organization? As stewards, we must understand His standards for operating His organization. We cannot create our own. We must resist setting our own standards because they typically are not the same as God's.

Recall in Acts 4:19 when Peter and John are brought in front of the council and told to stop speaking about Jesus. They replied "Do you think God wants us to obey you rather than him? We cannot stop telling about everything we have seen and heard." What great enthusiasm! This statement is just as applicable to us as leaders today. The world wants us to obey them rather than God. The world wants us to focus on self, materialism, legalism, looks, image, self-help introspection and reliance on Oprah, Dr. Phil, "the stars," or "the forces of nature" or "the universe" for our wisdom. They want us to refuse to acknowledge that God is alive, sovereign and will hold people accountable for their sins against the Holy Spirit (i.e., denying the saving reality and existence of Jesus). Peter and John had it right – they sought to do what was right in God's eyes rather than what was right in man's eyes.

Once the vision and plans are being executed, we must determine how God wants us to steward the resulting revenue and profits. Obviously, some of the revenue must be used to pay the suppliers we hire to generate the product or service we offer. Some of the revenue must be used to pay the employees who receive our direction and who are relying on us for their livelihood. After paying all expenses, we must ask the Owner what He wants us to do with the money that is left over. Should we keep it as the manager's bonus? Or is some of it better off being invested in the organization for growth? Or in the community for renewal or outreach? Or for the staff for their development? Or to advance the Kingdom?

We are called to love God with all our heart, soul, mind and strength. (Mark 12:30) This applies to our behavior as stewards of what He rightfully owns. Running the organization as if it were ours is not honoring God. This behavior is self-centered. Being God-centered is evidenced by loving God with all our heart, soul, mind and strength. Our motivation cannot be for our benefit or the benefit of our families or investors. Our motivation must be for the benefit of the Owner. The Owner has proven over and over and over again that He is faithful in providing for our needs if we are faithful in doing what He asks us to do.

As we accept our role as stewards of organizations that God owns, we must also accept that our purpose is to glorify the real owner of the organization. When we look to see what Jesus told His followers to do, one of the most important directives is what we call the Great Commission found in Matthew 28:19-20 (NKJV). Jesus commands His disciples, "Go therefore and make disciples of all the nations, baptizing them in the name of the Father and of the Son and of the Holy Spirit, teaching them to observe all things that I have commanded you ..." One of the most important purposes of our organization must be to make disciples.

We can do this in a variety of ways. A church organization plays a direct role in fulfilling this commission. They preach the word, baptize new Christians and provide discipleship (teaching and edifying) opportunities through Sunday School, home groups, or other forms of learning. With part of the congregation's offering, they support missionaries either locally or abroad to help preach the Word. They coordinate mission trips for young people and adults to model and share the Word.

Business organizations play both direct roles (holding Bible studies, praying in the workplace, etc.) and indirect roles by funding other organizations that can help fulfill this commission. Business organizations must be intentional about their role. They cannot look at the year end financial results and then determine what they will do to support the Great Commission. They must commit to this upfront as they allocate for any other budgeted item.

My friend Jim Dismore operates an organization called Kingdom Way Companies. On their website is the statement, "God never intended that our spiritual lives, our personal lives, and our business lives should be lived independently of each other and yet that is the reality in much of the business world." One of the key purposes of this organization is to help businesses integrate all three lives. One aspect of this is to encourage business leaders to have a ministry plan as part of the business, whereby the business identifies a particular ministry to be actively engaged with, support financially and be able to contribute to the Great Commission. Jim recommends the ministry plan be integrated with the business plan. He also recommends the ministry plan be fully communicated to the employees so they can become engaged with the plan.

God will test us with little to determine if we can be trusted with larger responsibilities. As I shared in the *Leadership Development* chapter, our character must be better developed than our talent. If our character is weak, we will likely fail in our responsibilities as they become greater because we will allow our pride, ego, greed and self-centeredness to take a greater place in our lives. Weak character causes us to fail the test resulting in God calling us wicked and lazy, as the master did to the third slave in the parable. Notice that he was called wicked and lazy because he knew the master's requirements and expectations, but still did not follow them.

As stewards of organizations that belong to God, we are accountable for developing like-minded leaders who can take over our role in due time. We are accountable for ensuring the next generation of leaders who buy into the vision, mission and core values that have been established.

If we are thinking of selling the business, we are accountable for transitioning it to a like-minded organization or individual(s) who will continue to operate the organization for God's purposes and will continue to treat employees, customers and vendors like you have in the past. Does your exit plan account for this type of transition? Simply pursuing the American dream and selling a business to the highest bidder when it seems most financially optimal for you reflects a self-centered agenda and not a God-centered agenda. He cares just as much about who follows a CEO as He does who follows a Christ-centered senior pastor. Selling a Christian company that is doing effective business as ministry to a non-believing owner comes at a great eternal price.

As Christian leaders, we are called to know God's requirements and expectations. We are managers of what He has provided us, and yes, this does include the organization where we lead others. We have a responsibility to use all the talents (time, ability, skills, and financial resources) He has provided in a way that furthers His purposes and His kingdom. We cannot squander any of these talents on self-centered or self-focused activities. Our decision-making lens must be God-centered.

God provides each one of us with a unique set and combination of talents. He calls us to use these unique talents for the furtherance of His Kingdom, not for our pleasure. It is not a matter of how much He has given us. It is a matter of what we do with what He has given to us. This is an important point. God is the one who can multiply, not us. We must be faithful in what God has provided so He can multiply and therefore grow His Kingdom. If we were able to multiply it, then we could take credit for its growth. God has designed it so He receives the credit. We are to allow Him to use us, so He can do the multiplication and He alone can receive the glory.

Self Assessment

Below are twenty statements that are indicative of an organization, department or leader who has accepted their role as a steward, not owner, within the organization. As you read the statements, be aware of the first response that comes to mind for you OR the organization and circle the number in the appropriate column.

Never – 1	Seldom – 2	Sometimes – 3	Usually – 4	Always – 5

1. Our organization has a vision and mission statement that honors God.

         1   2   3   4   5

2. Our organization has a vision and mission statement acknowledging that God owns the organization.

         1   2   3   4   5

3. When I read that God owns everything, I understand that means my organization as well.

         1   2   3   4   5

4. Major decisions are made taking into account that God is the owner of this organization and we (or I) seek to satisfy His plans and purposes.

         1   2   3   4   5

5. In making decisions, I seek first His kingdom.

         1   2   3   4   5

6. I am an active member of a Christ-centered business leader group that meets on a frequent basis to learn God's expectations of me as His steward.

         1   2   3   4   5

Stewardship

7. I have regular and frequent quiet time to be alone with God, to read His word as a way to understand His plans for the work He has called me to do.

     1   2   3   4   5

8. I have a practice of getting away at least once a quarter to have alone time with God and reflect on my progress against His plans for this organization and/or to reflect on my role in this organization.

     1   2   3   4   5

9. I have a strong desire to hear Jesus tell me, "Well done good and faithful servant" when I meet Him.

     1   2   3   4   5

10. I lean toward being God-centered in the decisions I make in this organization.

     1   2   3   4   5

11. I have experienced tests of faithfulness so God can determine my level of commitment.

     1   2   3   4   5

12. The priorities I have for the organization are fully aligned with God's priorities for this organization.

     1   2   3   4   5

13. I fully acknowledge that I am a steward of the employees God has placed under my leadership.

     1   2   3   4   5

14. I fully acknowledge that I am a steward of the financial resources at my disposal.

     1   2   3   4   5

15. Our organization has a ministry plan that is integrated into the business plan.

     1   2   3   4   5

16. I have turned away from (or recommended the organization turn away from) opportunities that, while appearing lucrative, were not in the best interests of the Owner.

1   2   3   4   5

17. Our organization has targeted specific resources to help advance the Kingdom.

1   2   3   4   5

18. Our organization has an intentional plan to do our part in carrying out the Great Commission.

1   2   3   4   5

19. I have taken the necessary steps to develop like-minded leaders to follow me so the organization is prepared to carry on without me.

1   2   3   4   5

20. I regularly discuss the responsibility of being a steward with those leaders underneath me.

1   2   3   4   5

Total your score here: _____

If you scored between 80 and 100 – Congratulations, you have accepted your role as a steward and are behaving accordingly. Well done!

If you scored between 60 and 79 – You have made some great progress, yet have a way to go before truly having the heart of a steward.

If you scored under 60 – You are encouraged to take the necessary steps as outlined in this chapter to develop the heart of a steward and to be more God-centered in your leadership role.

Practical Steps to Exhibit Stewardship

1. Take time to review your vision and mission to determine if they both honor God and acknowledge that the organization is His.
2. Develop a ministry plan that is funded and focuses on spreading the Gospel in some way.
3. Allow time for unhurried quiet time and prayer to determine if the vision, purpose and current key initiatives are appropriate in light of your role as a steward, not an owner.
4. Take regular and scheduled time to reflect on whether your priorities, both in the organization as well as outside, are aligned with God's priorities given your role as a steward for what He has given you.
5. Start a list of prayer requests that anyone in the organization can contribute to and commit to prayer on a regular basis.
6. Commit to join a group like FCCI, C12 Group or a similar organization. If one is not currently in operation in your area, pray about starting one for you and other Christian leaders in your community.
7. Reflect on the current policies you or your organization practice in terms of treatment of employees. Are they appropriate for a steward of God's organization? Change what you can so they are in line with what God would expect.
8. Ensure that each employee under your supervision has a targeted development plan in place designed to maximize the use of the talents God has provided them whether they are Christian or not.
9. Reflect on the current policies you or your organization practice in terms of treatment of customer and supplier. Are they appropriate for a steward of God's organization? Change what you can so they are in line with what God would expect.
10. Reflect on the current policies you or your organization practice in terms of the impact you have on the communities where you operate. Are they appropriate for a steward of

God's organization? Change what you can so they are in line with what God would expect.

11. Commit to be actively engaged in developing the next generation of leaders in a manner that is reflective of a steward.

12. Commit to be actively engaged in sharing the principles of stewardship to the current and next generation of leaders.

13. Establish a weekly time of reflection on your activities and ask the question, "If God appeared to me today to coach me on those activities, would He say, 'Well done, good and faithful servant'?"

14. Identify any decisions you have recently made that were not aligned with God's intentions for your organization and resolve to change those decisions to the best of your ability.

15. Re-examine the intended uses of any anticipated profits for this year. Are those plans aligned with and in the best interest of the true Owner of the organization?

16. Consider forming an advisory board for you or your organization that will help to hold you accountable for your role as a steward.

17. Consider identifying a mentor for you who can hold you accountable for your role as a steward.

18. Consider how important it is for you to receive worldly praise. As appropriate, resolve to focus more on receiving praise from God rather than humans.

19. Make a careful evaluation of those from whom you seek advice. Looking at these people through God's criteria – are they among the wise or are they fools? Resolve to make appropriate adjustments.

20. Make a careful assessment as to whose advice you are following. If you lean more toward what the world values, make appropriate changes in the sources of information you seek to gain wisdom and information. Resist the temptation to do what is right in your own eyes.

FINAL THOUGHTS

It is quite clear to me that the world needs more leaders who are truly committed to practicing leadership based on reliable biblical truths. It is also very evident that the vast majority of today's leaders are significantly lacking in their knowledge and application of Scriptural principles when it comes to leadership. This poses a serious deficiency in leadership and if left unchecked, can only become worse. Many of the biblical leaders profiled in this book were not perfect. They learned lessons as they went along. One thing they all did well was trust God and follow His direction. They were also very knowledgeable of the Scriptures. I hope that you have been encouraged by reading the leadership lessons.

God has work for Christian leaders to perform that He has identified and called us to do. He will equip those leaders He calls and who are committed to carry out these tasks in the manner He prescribes. He has placed (and will continue to place) people in leadership positions to accomplish His purposes. As II Chronicles 16:9 says, He has been looking "throughout the earth to strengthen those whose hearts are fully committed to Him." Are you one of those people He has called into a leadership position? Will you answer His call and humbly say "Here I am Lord, send me"?

Does He expect our performance to be perfect? Hardly, yet He does expect us to follow His formula for providing leadership to those He has placed under our authority, regardless of whether or not we are part of a Christian-run organization.

As I mentioned in the Preface, I suggest that you review the notes you highlighted in each chapter indicating the practical steps you might take to develop the necessary behaviors and habits of God-designed leaders. Based on years of personal experience, I am a firm believer that new habits take a long time to take hold. I have also been a believer that a person can only reasonably work on one, two or maximum three new habits at a time. Based on this, I strongly encourage you to identify the one, two or three practical steps that may have the most impact on your leadership.

It is great that you are motivated to want to change and improve. It is also probably a good assumption that you are an extremely busy leader with large demands on your time. Before you commit to adding some new things to do, I strongly encourage you to identify one, two or three things that you currently spend time doing, and decide to either delegate or drop those activities. It makes no sense to continually add things to your crowded agenda without taking things off that agenda to make room for more impactful activities. If you only add activities, you will find it very difficult to truly devote the time necessary to transform the new activities into effective habits. You will lose motivation for continuing and realize that nothing has changed. Instead, commit to drop some things before taking on the new things.

If some of your chosen activities involve changing your personal leadership habits, you are encouraged to commit to practice the new behaviors or habits for a minimum of forty-five days. This will allow the habits to take shape, become engrained in your normal base of other habits and truly make the habit comfortable. The first few times you try the new habit, it will most likely feel uncomfortable. If the new habit involves some public display, the people who observe you are likely to give you some funny looks. This is alright – expect it and stick with it until you start to see the positive results that will come.

Some of you may be considering placing this material into the hands and minds of your leadership team. For this purpose, there is a *Leadership Lessons from THE BOOK* workshop available for you and your team. The workshop is complete with workbooks and extended materials. It can be customized to be completed in one or two days, or through several weeks or months in a shorter module format. For further information, please contact me via www.blissassociates.com.

Bliss & Associates Inc.

Advisory Services to Cultivate Exceptional Leadership

Since 1996 we have been assessing, coaching, developing and equipping leaders with the competencies, disciplines and practical tools needed to succeed in leadership and life. Contact us today to discuss how we can help you maximize your leadership potential and train up the next generation of leaders in your organization.

Services Include:

Leadership Assessment
One-On-One Executive Coaching
On-Boarding Coaching and Program Design
Organizational Assessment
Culture and Opinion Surveys
Strategic Planning and Meeting Facilitation
Customized Leadership Development Workshops
Employee Retention Services
Leadership Lessons from THE BOOK Workshops

If you want to provide the key concepts contained in this book to the leadership team in your organization and truly enable them to be the leaders God has called them to be contact us today to discuss the *Leadership Lessons from THE BOOK* Workshop that can be provided at your location.

Contact us at www.blissassociates.com

ABOUT THE AUTHOR

WILLIAM G BLISS

Bill is a leadership consultant with more than twenty-five years of experience providing advice and guidance to leaders across a wide variety of organizations including public, private, family-run, non-profit, church and ministry organizations. He has designed and conducted leadership training workshops, provided executive coaching, and developed leadership assessment and succession planning tools for many organizations across the United States. Since 1996, he has led a consulting firm and has been blessed with organizational and individual clients who desire to maximize their leadership gifts and talents. He and his wife currently live near Greenville, South Carolina and are active members in their church. He can be contacted through www.blissassociates.com.